Social Media and Small Business Marketing

By Stephen Wilson

ISBN: 1453824693

EAN-13: 9781453824696

Printed by: University Business Printing
& Press – United States of America

Introduction

Social Media marketing does not have to be overwhelming, mysterious, or immeasurable, as a promotional tactic for small business. Most business books about social media marketing tend to focus on the variety and types of online media (Facebook, Twitter et al), instead of focusing on developing Social Media marketing plans. It's no wonder that small business is reluctant to get involved with social media. It seems most Social Media marketing books have lost their business focus and adopted a simple mantra: *Be everywhere and do everything* – Online videos! Podcasts! Blogs! Mobile Marketing! Those are impossible, meaningless recommendations for a small business owner already overwhelmed with responsibilities.

Social Media marketing should be measureable

The process of developing workable Social Media plans relies less on utilizing multiple Social Media outlets and more on developing marketing goals appropriate for this promotional channel that measurably improve profits. Any new marketing initiative, including Social Media, should be incorporated seamlessly into existing business objectives.

Additionally, like any other promotional channel, a campaign should produce results that are quantifiable upon completion or at milestones along the way. Developing a plan with built-in metrics gives your project energy and momentum; for if you really knew you could reach your customers and measure your success; would you still be ambivalent about pursuing Social Media marketing?

Any type of marketing effort should make business sense. Far too many business people get caught up in the Social Media hype, and begin to believe they need a "Facebook strategy." Well, there is no such thing as a Facebook strategy; Facebook is only a tool. Your business may be helped by a marketing strategy that has Social Media (with possibly Facebook) as a promotional tactic, but no business should decide to invest resources with any online application simply because of that site's popularity. It would be the equivalent of a homebuilder creating a "hammer strategy" due to the hammer's ranking as a favorite construction tool.

In truth, most small business people feel a certain amount of "push" and "pull" about Social Media. They have heard the hoopla and read the breathless stories. Stunning case studies abound in the current crop of Social Media marketing books. These sagas often profile a bootstrap marketer climbing from obscurity to national success through adept Social Media marketing. Although these stories are engaging, a typical small business owner needs something far more direct and real than a case study. He or she wants to know – Is Social Media marketing a good choice for my business, in my city, and with my customers? Helping you answer that question is the mission of this book.

Small business has advantages in Social Media

Social Media provides two big marketing advantages to small businesses as the medium both leverages and magnifies your existing business strengths. Your first advantage is the size of your market. It is far easier to locate and target prospects in a defined area compared to a broad national campaign. Second, Social Media tends to level the playing field between competitors of unequal size. That should be welcomed news in today's hyper-competitive business world, since larger corporations frequently have a more favorable position in terms of scale and resources.

How does Social Media level the competitive landscape? Because it plays by a different, more personal set of rules. One example: **online consumer reviews**, captured on services such as Yelp, City Search or other local search engines. Many of these Sites feature performance reviews that are the traditional strengths of small business; personalized service, product knowledge, and transaction ease. Posts from shoppers often become unpaid but very effective promotions with real business value. Both market research and sales results indicate that customer reports and rankings of product quality and service transactions play a key role in influencing purchasing decisions. Mobile shopper's reports and Social Media are growing in importance for small business success.

Additionally, Social Media highlights the most powerful asset of any small business – the owner. Social Media allows you to engage with your customers in the most personal and productive manner available to business marketing.

As I mentioned above, Social Media cannot do anything for your business if you implement it as an initiative by itself; but correctly incorporated into your overall business planning it can have significant impact. Here is a short list of possible goals for a Social Media campaign:

- Gain new customers, increase sales
- Build store or Website traffic
- Enhance customer loyalty, encourage repeat purchases, promote customer referrals
- Develop new products or services, simplify market tests and surveys
- Increase the perceived value of your products and enhance customer service

How to use this book

To benefit from this book, you don't need a great deal of previous knowledge of Social Media and the many, many Websites that are part of this online phenomenon. It is much more important to develop an organized planning process that leads to the technology choice, rather than relying on the technology to create a marketing plan. As the business owner, you should be in control.

Section One – Understanding Social Media and marketing

This section defines and describes the world of Social Media, free from jargon and techno-speak. It is a medium full of contradictions, risks and rewards. For a communication channel that prides itself on the simple concept of enabling "conversations", it can be surprisingly complex. Keeping your focus on your individual business goals, however, can clarify your thinking.

Section Two - Building a marketing plan

Building a small business plan for Social Media is built on a simple triad, customized in the following manner:

- You – your abilities, interests, and time
- Your business – its strengths, weaknesses, competition, brand identity, and keeping your overall marketing plan coherent. Also, your competitors and local business environment
- Your customers – How do they currently use Social Media? How to seek and engage them.

Most importantly, this section explains traditional marketing metrics that will help you track results and quantify the value (your ROI) of every customer you acquire from your hard work.

Section Three - Social Media – tools and resources

When you reach this point in the book, you will know much more about yourself and Social Media and you will have a good idea of which tools are suitable for you, your business and customers. To assist in your planning, I profile the most prominent Social Media tools such as Facebook, Twitter, Foursquare and others, including each application's business strategy and development.

As an added bonus, I have developed a list of about 200 online tools (most are free) that will help you refine your Social Media marketing efforts, locate your customers and prospects, and track your brand online.

Should you be involved in Social Media? I can't answer that question from this distance, but *you* will be able to make an informed decision upon completing this book. You will have a clear understanding of Social Media marketing for small business. You'll also know how your best customers and prospects are using Social Media. Even better, you'll know how to build a plan that produce metrics that make business sense.

With that knowledge in your grasp, your possible involvement with Social Media is an easier question to answer. You will be able to forecast its potential for *your* business, in *your market.*

Table of Contents

Section One: Understanding Social Media

1. Social Media and Small Business Marketing

   Definitions and examples of Social Media can be broad and include dissimilar elements such as customer reviews, micro-blogs, video and location-based services. How Social Media should be incorporated into an existing small business plan.

2. A Brief History of Social Media

   The rise of user-generated content and social networking began in the earliest days of the Web and became the virtual center of Web engagement. Today, some form of Social Media is part of almost every Website.

3. Rise of the Micro-blogs

   How Twitter, Facebook and My Space grew to dominate this media, while marketers still struggle to find their role.

4. Location-Based Social Media marketing

Social media is new, but still-newer location-based applications, such as Foursquare and others are already changing the social media landscape and challenging the dominance of market leaders.

5. Illustrations

Images and screenshots.

Section Two: Building a Social Media Marketing Plan

Social Media is full of contradictions that should guide your thinking. Marketing plans should be built on a triad that reflects your understanding of You, Your Business, and Your Customers.

6. Different Ways to Look at Social Media

An essay describing the many contradictions inherent in Social Media; it can be free of cost, but expensive in terms of time. These contradictions illustrate opportunities and risks for your business.

7. Developing a Business Plan for You, Your Business, and Your Customers

Every business has different strengths and weaknesses; what are your value messages that translate into effective Social Media messages? Your most profitable customers and finding Social Media examples that are useful for your business.

8. Determining Profit from Social Media Marketing

What's the return on your Social Media investment? Grouping online customers by demographics and profitability is the key to determining potential profits.

Section Three: Tools and Resources

Major Social Media applications in-depth with tools and resources.

9. Twitter
10. Facebook
11. LinkedIn
12. YouTube
13. Foursquare
14. Online Resources

The abundance of online resources, almost 200 Social Media sites will help you find your customers, measure your effectiveness, and improve your performance.

Chapter One

Social Media and Small Business Marketing

It is difficult to define Social Media in a manner that everyone readily accepts. Perhaps it is because the Social Media spectrum is so broad that the media can include such disparate features as anonymous customer reviews, business blogs, and even a customer winning the title of "mayor" at the local dry cleaners. Still, it is helpful in any book about Social Media to begin with a shared understanding of both the media and the marketing that surrounds it. So, exactly what is Social Media?

A Definition of Social Media

Social Media includes any of the many online tools that allow people with similar interests to share information, learn from others, or network in an open process. The information found on these sites is commonly referred to as "user-generated content", which means that anyone is able to post to the site with minimal restrictions or oversight. This user-supplied content can vary widely in form as written posts, photos, videos, original music, or bookmarked links. It can be unstructured; such as family photos on Facebook, or very detailed and formal, such as articles on Wikipedia.

A partial list of the structuring possibilities of a Social Media site could include any combination of forums, blogs, micro-blogs, photo-sharing, video-sharing, bookmark-sharing, online publishing, customer reviews, professional and social networking, or any more-traditional Website structure that accepts posts from an unstructured, online community. The media has become such an important element in driving views and page visits that some sort of Social Media feature is found almost anywhere you land on the Web.

It is important to note that the veracity of the content placed on Social Media outlets is not vetted. *This may be its defining characteristic.* It reflects the broad spectrum of humankind. It can be insightful or dull, balanced or biased, guarded or too revealing, and most importantly, verifiably true or outrageously libelous. Accurate or false, anything can be posted online with either the best of intentions or with malicious intent. Perhaps it is this unpredictability that makes for such compelling reading. In any event, it becomes the ongoing challenge for online readers to gauge the relative importance and validity of what they discover.

Social media applications and Websites are so numerous across the Web, it is probably impossible to list all the possible variations. A simple list of some basic Social Media formats follows:

Blogs: Originally termed "Web logs", blogs began as personal reflections capturing family events or hobbies and interests, but very quickly, blogs were adapted to meet professional and business goals.

Although there are a myriad of blog software and Websites, both free and paid, **WordPress** software is one of the most versatile platforms for blogs – especially blogs intended for marketing promotions. According to WordPress, there have been over 100 million downloads of their software.

Micro-Blogs: Short postings, limited in scope and time-demands on users have become very popular. The daunting challenge of creating readable essays for a blog is made easier by the design of these short-format outlets. The notable competitors in micro-blogs include **Twitter**, **Facebook**, and **My Space**.

Mobile and Local Search Engines: When you go to the Web, either on your Mobile phone or your home PC, to find a local dry cleaners or Italian restaurant, it is likely you'll first be directed to a site that lists the businesses that meet your search criteria in your area. It's an important sales funnel, and competitors like **Google Places**, **Bing**, **Yahoo Local**, **Yelp** and many others have created local business search engines to capture this growing search field. It is user-generated content, however; that makes these sites valuable via online customer reviews. Is the barbeque served at "Jake's Place" good? Google doesn't have a clue, but the locals know for sure.

Customer Reviews Everywhere: Most online stores now include some type of customer product review feature. Frequent reviewers on some sites are given prominence and can develop their own "followers". Examples of product reviews can be found on **Amazon** and **L.L. Bean**.

Bookmarking Sites: For folks with a niche interest, bookmarking sites allow you to leverage the knowledge of like-minded people to discover Websites or businesses catering to your interests. **Digg** and **StumbleUpon** are examples of prominent bookmark sites.

Video: Everyone knows **YouTube**, but there is more to video on the Web than cute kitties. Many businesses are using videos to provide added-value features such as instructional videos, educational podcasts, or marketing videos.

Podcasts: Podcasts can range from Webcam videos to online radio, with production values sometimes soaring upward to match traditional broadcast standards. Both **YouTube** and the online **Apple** store offer podcasts. Although very popular, the rising quality of productions makes it increasingly difficult to easily enter this market – unless you are targeting a niche field with little direct competition.

Photo-sharing: You can post your photos for the world to see or keep them private for family or friends. **Flickr** is only one site that will post your photos.

Location-based Media: New Social Media applications let you "check in" online to your local restaurant or bar and receive rewards or badges for frequent visits. Who knew that becoming the "mayor" of the local diner would be such a big deal? One of the growing competitors in this arena is **Foursquare**. What isn't known, however; is if or when user-privacy becomes an issue with location-based Social Media.

Networking Sites: Perhaps there is a new truism in this digital age: It is not who you know, but who you can link to that is most important for job advancement. Certainly this is true on sites like **LinkedIn**, where business professionals try to connect with friends and former associates to boost their career prospects. LinkedIn is also a great source to find out what works in Social Media marketing.

User-Created Content Sites: As the term implies, Websites such as **Wikipedia**, **eHow**, **Associated Content**, and many others, allow users to write articles, review products, produce videos, or post essays on their site. These types of sites allow any content creator to leverage the Web host's existing high authority with Google and potentially reach a Web audience that ranges into the millions.

This list covers the main outlets, but is not comprehensive. Also, some of these Sites feature multiple types of Social Media; reviews and bookmarks, for example. As technology advances, we are sure to see new applications that are not possible today. As a result of this ever-shifting landscape, defining Social Media *marketing* is as challenging as defining the media itself, but let us try to do so.

Social Media marketing

Social Media marketing is a promotional activity whereby a business targets customers or prospects through Social Media sites in an effort to increase sales, strengthen brand loyalty, or achieve other business goals. It is unlike traditional promotional marketing which depends upon purchased placement on high-traffic Medias such as television or print.

In contrast, a marketing position on many Social Media sites is frequently available for no direct charge to a business in terms of paid placement, but requires a marketer to devise a method to attract interest by providing information or resources that are judged by the targeted audience as offering value. This perceived value, which generates views or return visits, is typically separate, but should be ultimately congruent with the business's traditional products or service lines. For example, "tweeting" your restaurant's daily specials can provide value to nearby office workers struggling with gaining consensus on their lunch plans.

A Social Media marketing plan can take many forms, a business may create a page on Facebook; or develop a thoughtful blog focusing on issues relating to its business segment; or use newer tools like Foursquare and reward return visits to a brick and mortar location with virtual badges. Almost anything digital is possible. Even with this variety, all Social Media marketing focuses on a traditional marketing goal – increased profitability for the business.

Easier said than done, the marketing challenge of providing content that attracts viewers and impacts customer behavior is difficult to achieve. Social Media marketing is often criticized for engaging in activities which create many "views", but does little to improve business financials in a transparent and measureable manner. Without a clear link between resource expenditures and economic return, the marketing value of Social Media will always remain uncertain. To avoid this pitfall, always pursue strategies that can produce measureable results.

Chapter Two

A Brief History of Social Media

A great many businesses are certain that they must build a robust social media presence. This assumption has become so ingrained, in fact, that few challenge it. It seems that no matter what kind of industry in which you are involved, there is a drive towards social media. It is almost an understatement to say that Social Media is a hot topic, and it is easy to understand why that is. Featured stories in virtually every business publication tout this "new" form of online exchange as an innovative (and free!) way to increase sales or strengthen a brand.

But before a productive Social Media discussion can begin, however, it helps to have a clear understanding of how "social media", not only permeates the Web, but cannot, in fact, be separated from almost any portion of popular Web exchange, whether for business or pleasure. Since this book focuses on the business applications for small business of popular social media tools, it's important to understand that Social Media developed without broad, cross-functional business applications in mind.

The Beginning

Although most people automatically think of Social Media through the lens of sites like Facebook and Twitter, the development of the media is much broader - and has a longer history. In fact, a form of social media was present at the beginning, when the public first accessed the Internet in the 1990's. At its core, the Internet has always been about social interaction.

The notion that Social Media constitutes a new organism on the Internet just isn't accurate. The Web has always been about people around the world with similar interests congregating and exchanging ideas. In short, the Internet has always been about socializing and communication. Social Media has just changed the formula and the packaging.

Online Forums

Thus, we need to ask ourselves what those early days of the Internet looked like. If we glance backwards, we can easily see that many of the functional elements that we see today were also available during the web's initial years.

In those early days of the Web, a rudimentary structuring of social interaction began through "forums", which allowed users to post messages and create an online dialogue linked by conversation "threads". This new digital communication channel, although primitive by today's standards, gave millions of people an easy, affordable, and more importantly, popular way to "publish" their own ideas, thoughts, and beliefs, to a wider online audience. The fact that this structure of social interaction was simple does not negate its power. The example of online forums illuminates the point that from its very inception, the Internet has been largely constructed around the basic but powerful idea of fostering interaction.

Of course, this is not to state that these rudimentary structures of social interaction resembled the Social Media of today. Clearly, that is not the case. While the core functionality of interaction was present, it was positively primordial when compared to the Social Media we all currently enjoy.

In comparison, most Websites of that time were little more than electronic brochures, containing static, unchanging "pages". Forums, however, with their lively user-contributions; were always interesting, and continually refreshed, providing new and sometimes controversial content. It made for great reading, but it was also social media in its mewing infancy. That stated, however, it is important to acknowledge the contribution of these simple websites as they helped point to what would ultimately be possible. Indeed these early efforts did wonders to spark the imagination and lay the foundation for what would come.

Blogs - Social Media's First Steps

The year 2001 marked a major turning point for Social Media. By then, the broader possibilities of the Web were explored by a new concept, first called Weblogs, and then shortened to "blogs". Blogs replaced the cluttered forums, providing a way to create a single, more-focused communication channel. Blogs made it easy to post commentary on any subject and develop an audience of like-minded readers that replied to the blogger's posts, adding to, and enlivening the content. Although most of these early blogs centered on family activities, others began to focus on topics such as politics and business, and some lucky bloggers found themselves with an online audience numbering in the thousands. This newfound ease of use and the open nature of the blog format combined in a synergistic fashion to create a new twist on Internet based communication. As it turned out, this new twist was one that was well received to say the least.

Blogs continued to grow over the next few years as their interactive nature appealed to users and blog creators alike. However, this is not to state that everyone instantly recognized and embraced the potential of blogs. In fact, the opposite was often the case.

When blogs first appeared, corporations were leery of the new medium, but by January of 2005, Fortune magazine was forced to encourage business leaders to capitulate to the inevitable, in a cover story entitled, "Why You Can't Ignore Bloggers". Bloggers, and by extension their readers, were American consumers, ignore them at your own peril. Corporate America may not have liked it, but online communication channels were giving consumers new power to shape products and pricing. Realizing that a major avenue of communication and expression was being ignored, many corporations sat up and took notice of the humble blog. Soon it occurred to many corporate executives that perhaps a better corporate strategy would be to join, rather than avoid, online conversations with consumers, the article suggested.

In hindsight, perhaps the most noteworthy aspect of the blog was its role in demonstrating the new, but still raw power of individuals to create a group of online "followers" without the support or the added legitimacy provided by a political position or professional title. While we may take this for granted today, the fact is that the potential power and influence of the blog was something new. It is safe to also state that the blog was transformative as well. The blog, with its ability to cheaply and easily attract visitors, was profoundly different from the modes of communication that preceded it. The Internet gave anyone and everyone a chance to build an audience, and depending on their singular abilities exert influence in just about all areas of human endeavor.

Product Reviews – Courting the Social Researchers

Faced with the proposition of losing out on this emerging form of interactive communications; corporations entered unfamiliar territory. They began to slowly relinquish control of all online content relating to their business or product in order to utilize the emerging strength of customer-sourced product reviews. These reviews, typically placed adjacent to a product on a Web storefront, were demonstrating an unexpected ability to influence consumer purchasing behavior.

In 2004, Amazon became one of the first high-profile companies to accept user-generated reviews of books and other products. These ratings soon became a powerful tool in driving sales. Once again, the Web showed that average people can have a more influential voice on the Web than experts; in Amazon's case, book critics, from major media outlets. Stating that this was a bit of a shock to the system within certain circles is a profound understatement.

Other companies followed quickly Amazon's example. In some of these product review applications, visitors could also "subscribe" to their favorite reviewer's posts, allowing the reviewer to build his own audience. This is a theme that we will return to later: The emerging role of "influencers" in purchase decisions. In the sometimes bizarre world of Social Media, your most important customer may not be a large customer at all. The good news is that small business is well-positioned to build a marketing strategy that recognizes the clout of these new influencers on a local level.

Yet all of this history does cause a number of questions to emerge. For example, why do people seem to prefer the opinions of relatively anonymous sources than working professionals in major media outlets? Perhaps it is similar to the distrust of "mainstream media" that is frequently heard in political discussions. There have been occasions when the impartial nature of media-sourced product reviews has been questioned. For example, in April of 2010, in an article entitled, "Apple IPad: The Reviews Are In," Fortune magazine noted that all of the new Apple IPad reviewers were handpicked by Steve Jobs, all, it continued, were from publications developing an IPad app and stood to profit from the IPad.

Perhaps a certain segment of the population wants the feedback of those that they feel are more like them. Having the opinion of someone that is more on the level of a peer, whose status in life and socio-economic background is more likely to mirror their own, is often deemed preferable over an expert. Further, it may be stories like the Steve Jobs-IPod story relayed above that prompts many to cultivate an overall distrust of major media outlets.

Whatever the reason, the authority of online reviews is real. In 2007, a research project commissioned by Power Reviews quantified the influence of online product reviews. According to the study, people who utilized online reviews to make purchasing decisions were identified as "social researchers". The study found that 65% of online shoppers said they "always" read online reviews before making a decision. An example from this report highlighted a company called Delightful Deliveries, which added customer reviews to its Website and found, within two months, a 20% increase in conversion rates among products receiving four and five star reviews.

Video

For many years, limited bandwidth made adding videos to the Web impractical. As the speed of the Internet increased, however, video uploading became a practically alternative. Once again, however; most businesses failed to see the possibilities of video until You Tube exploded onto the market in 2005. The quality of videos seemed irrelevant as millions of viewers were transfixed by videos of ninja kitties, dancing babies, and proto-millionaires promoting their products via their computer's built-in Web cam. Along with the amateur videos, new promotional opportunities arose on YouTube for traditional businesses, large and small. Today, YouTube is one of many video sharing sites that allow face to face communication with customers on a 24/7 basis. It now rivals its parent, Google, for the number of online searches each year. Social Media is multi-media.

Mobile Marketing

In the first days of the Web, the Internet was only reluctantly accepted as a required marketing tool by small business. In an already over-booked day, some small business owners saw little need for Internet marketing, especially since they thought most of their business success was due to their original choice of location, word of mouth referrals, and the local yellow pages. When these small enterprises finally came online, they chose a URL that reflected a company name, but did little to support their online discovery.

As Google and other search engines began to promote a new ability to perform location-based searches, it became apparent that companies needed to be gathered together both by location and business type to make local searches effective. New Web-enabled phones also provided the ability to both virtually shop for products and prices online and actively shop simultaneously in the real world. Companies like Yelp, City Search, Yahoo, Bing, Google and a host of other competitors, began courting this market by providing city-specific directories, or new search engine capabilities for location-based, product or service searches. But for smaller businesses, this new online service was confusing and mostly unwelcome. Many business owners had been slow to put their original company Website online and now discovered they were listed multiple times on local-oriented "mini-sites". Just how many hours in a day are there?

Are these online local shopping directories and search tools, social media? I believe they are. All of these new local and mobile search services actively solicit online reviews from customers. In major markets, a popular business might have dozens, if not hundreds, of reviews and counter-reviews across several sites that list that company. Yelp has proven to be particularly successful in gathering online customer critiques in major markets across the U.S. The comments from satisfied or angry customers, rightly or wrong, have been shown to be a major factor in determining customer purchase decisions.

Because of their measureable impact, online consumer ratings have become a significant issue. Their potential for harm reveals a very dark side to online customer reviews. Small businesses can be especially vulnerable to a few negative and anonymous reviews; but who vets the authenticity or accuracy of those ratings? For its part, Yelp has received criticism for approaching some of its customers and offering to remove the negative reviews - for a price.

In a May 17th, 2010 TechCrunch article entitled "Complaints against Yelp's 'Extortion' Practices Grow Louder," Leena Rao writes about a pending class action lawsuit against Yelp. The lawsuit alleged that the heavily funded startup runs an "extortion scheme" and has "unscrupulous sales practices" in place to generate revenue, in which the company's employees call businesses asking for monthly payments in the guise of advertising contracts, in exchange for removing or modifying negative reviews.

I do not think it is as simple as that. Yelp, perhaps more than any other local review company, understands the critical importance of customer comments. So, the question becomes, is monitoring customer posts and ratings a service or extortion? For small businesses located in the major markets that Yelp targets, a particularly scathing online post has the potential to effectively destroy a struggling business. So, now return to where we began, if it is not Yelp's role - or the other local search engines and sites such as Google or Bing, who is the arbiter of fairness in the sometimes combative, usually anonymous, world of online business reviews?

The growing importance of mobile search marketing via Web-enabled phones is just as, or more critical, for success than a business Facebook page or Twitter account. Ironically, mobile search sites and location-specific business directories are frequently ignored in discussions about Social Media.

Social Media Takes Center Stage

As technology and Web software continued to advance; the role of an online commentator was recognized, formalized, and became a standard Web design feature. Websites were just more interesting, and gained more traffic, when they allowed visitors to post comments, raise questions, or rate the quality of offered products and services. Again, just as we saw in the early days of the Internet, it is this aspect of interaction and interconnectivity that serves to attract users and audiences.

For companies, all of these factors overlap and combine in a rather interesting fashion; the power of followers or fans, product reviews and customer comments, was obvious. The question became; how best to profitably leverage the Social Media engine for practical business purposes?

My Space, Facebook, Twitter, LinkedIn, and so many more

Perhaps it was the explosive development of countless Social Media applications to make us think that something new had arisen on the Internet. If so, only our awareness is new. Today, a "social" tool is now part of virtually every site or blog. Again, many of the tools and applications may be new, but they tap into what was fundamentally attractive about the Internet to its users in the first place, namely connectivity and interactivity. Thus these tools represent further growth of what is at the very foundation of the Internet itself.

Ironically, as companies of all sizes debate on how to "get involved" with Social Media, it is a good bet that, unknowingly, they already are involved. How could they not be? If a business doesn't allow customer comments on its own Website, they will discover dozens of user-reviews on Yelp or City Search. If they search blogs and Twitter, they will find themselves there, too. LinkedIn? It probably features the resumes and activities of many of their employees.

The bottom line is that, like it or not, corporations are already social media animals. For large organizations, the sheer fact of their size inevitably means that they have a pronounced, albeit often de facto, presence. Smaller businesses are there, too. Just because a business is unaware of social media doesn't mean that it cannot either benefit or be hurt by the many varieties of online exchange.

At the beginning of the second decade of the 21st century, maybe we finally realize that we don't have something called "social media" that only exists in certain places on the Internet. Essentially social media is simply everywhere, and this fact is to only be expected as part of the on-going evolution of the Internet and its social aspects. Since the Internet has always been about communication and socialization, it should not surprise us that the tools have evolved as software and hardware increases in both power as well as sophistication.

Truly, we have a Social Web, with many new tools, and we are all a part of it. For small business, the key to success is to not be swayed by the compelling variety of online applications, and try to have a presence across the social media landscape, but to be front and center at the particular places of interest to you and your customers.

In most ways, the old rules of business still apply. You need to be where your customers are. This is a fundamental aspect of marketing, and is the same on the Web as it has always been in the more established forms of traditional media.

Chapter Three

Rise of the Microblogs

Twitter and Facebook may just be the name on everyone's lips, or more precisely at the tip of their fingers. But did you know that there are also Tumblr, Plurk, Emote. In, Beeing, identi.ca, Qaiku, Xing and Six Apart? If none of these sound familiar to you, then it's time to join the new wave, really a tsunami, of microblogging.

There are all sorts of interest tidbits about microblogs. Did you know the pioneering few were called tumbleblogs which first appeared in 2005? Not only have microblogs sprung up like wild mushrooms, supporting services to organize your microblogs have grown as well.

You have Lifestream that will efficiently collect all your microblogs from various social media websites. Doing exactly the opposite, Ping.fm will broadcast your micro-musings to multiple social networks.

What is a Microblog?

In Twitter's parlance, it's burst of texts in 140 characters or less. It could also be picture or video sharing, and in the case of Emote.In, it's sharing your emotions, or lifestreaming, over a discernible timeline.

Maybe the attraction of microblogging lies in the intellectual challenge of being able to capture a mood or a thought in 140 characters or less. To be a contemporary haiku poet.

Or maybe it's the adrenalin rush and the creative

high, according to recent studies, that come from dashing off a thought or an event, in the sure knowledge that somewhere in blogsphere, someone or multiple someones are reading your every Twitter.

Yes, microblogging has given rise to microcelebrities, and at anyone time, you can have 3,000 or 30,000 people reading about your latest shopping trip, your problems with the kids, uprisings in Iran or updates on terrorist attacks in Mumbai. And if the Vatican and various churches have their way, clergy and parishioners will be tweeting prayers and calls to faith.

Microblogging and the rise of Twitter has given rise to "prayer tweets" to create "a sea of prayer" to remind friends and family that they are being thought of, or to start conversations and ideas on sharing the faith. The Calvin Institute of Worship sets up various Twitter feeds to "pray the hours" in keeping with an ancient call to pray without ceasing.

The Different Faces of Microblogging Across the Globe

Stanford University uses its Facebook page to provide access to faculty and information about student projects, with a twist. Students can post questions for a specific professor on the Facebook Wall to be addressed by the faculty member during his assigned time on the wall.

Halfway across the globe in Japan, microblogging is being used by web-savvy housewives as an infowar weapon. Japanese housewives, minding their purses and in search of a bargain, have leveraged social media with military precision, to the despair of supermarket chains.

Everyday, an army of more than 25,000 "regional correspondents", or agents on the ground for the Mainichi Tokubai mobile website, scrutinize the sales of the day to find the cheapest offers available for their hundreds of thousands of users. Special offers, no matter how small, in more than 7,700 Japanese supermarkets come under the laser-sharp scrutiny of these consumer vigilantes who, through the power of social networking, get to knock ten yen or US$0.10 off a carton of milk.

The Brand is You

First, there was Generation X, then Y and now Z. The rapid pace of technology is creating "micro-generations" where even pre-teens are leaving teenagers behind in the dust with their ability to multi-task.

A study by California Professor, Larry Rosen show that digital natives (those who grew up with all things digital) between 16-18 can take on seven tasks such as checking social networking sites, texting, watching TV, emailing etc), eclipsing those in the 20s who can only handle 6 and those in their 30's who take on 5.5.

These are tomorrow's consumers, who in fact will influence the pattern of consumption for the next 50 years. With their need to stay connected, social networking and microblogging are definitely here to stay. And there is clearly a generation chasm about privacy and security. The younger digital natives are clearly not bothered about it. As Facebook puts it, "if you are not comfortable about sharing, don't."

These natives of Web 2.0 crave to be updated in real time – to be able to instantly check, track, map, judge and deliver verdicts on purchases and services. They rely heavily on peer reviews and they want self-focused content in a world where online status is developed from what you know and shared as an experience, rather than what you buy.

In the digital domain where you are the brand, an

unknown band can be bankrolled by its fans, even if it's just for gas money to the music festival in Austin.

New Rules of Engagement

Microblogging has changed the rules of engagement. We're now always broadcasting a message about ourselves, whether it be in tweets or updates to our Facebook profiles. It's the need to engage, to know that your voices are being heard and responded to, that has endeared Facebook and led to the proliferation of half a billion profiles.

MySpace blazed like wildfire when it was first introduced. However, due to cluttered design and constant technical problems, it impeded the engagement and destroyed the intimacy. Now, it has lost the popularity contest to the Facebook behemoth, shrinking into a music and entertainment social media site. The reason? Many perceive it as a place to creatively express yourself, whereas Facebook is a place that encourages a two way, or a multiple-way conversation.

Facebook has also shown itself to be fast on its feet in the brutally competitive world of social networks, by being able to innovate and keep things fresh and immediate.

How Businesses are Responding

Businesses are now seeing consumers as partners. Advertisers no longer tell just their story; it's now participation or citizen advertising, where companies work with consumers who blog about their experiences – good, bad or neutral.

In the world of commodity trading where knowledge is information, commodity traders, who make money on weather changes and crop numbers, are now following farmers' tweets about rainfall and latest crop yields. Fifth generation Nebraska farmer, Ryan Weeks, has more than 830 people following his tweets, far more than the entire population of his town.

In those places where speed saves lives, such as disaster relief organizations, social media is a weapon second to none in the length and width of its reach.

When Medical Teams International used Twitter to spread the news about the Haitian quake, it raised ten times the norm in donations on a single day. Social media gets the disaster pictures out quickly, brings home the full measure of tragedy, and leverages the social media networks of supporters and their followers. Altogether, a very potent relief response tool.

In the same spirit or reaching out to the collective intelligence, companies are now crowdsourcing, mass-collaborating, and co-creating with the very same consumers who buy their product.

Social Media: Engagement between Employee and Boss?

Is the new challenge facing companies to take social media within? Many corporations see the playful nature of social media as being counter-productive and time wasting. But isn't social media all about communication, and aren't corporate failures often due to failure to get the message through?

Social media is not just about the outside interaction between company and customer; it's also about the interaction within. Can social media be thought of as the new suggestion box?

Is there a place when social media can meet strategy? Will microblogging replace corporate email? Can microblogging be thought of as information crowdsourcing, information hubbing or information reuse? Enterprise microblogs such as Yammer, Communote and Status Net have been used successfully in small organizations with between 5-20 employees, and larger companies are starting to experiment.

Where is the Money?

All these seem very well and good. Small, nimble companies are using Twitter to level the playing field and establish a presence without being elbowed out by larger, richer companies which have more advertising dollars to spend.

Even Twitter, whose phenomenal popularity has really been shaped by the consumers themselves, is seeking to transform itself into a profitable business. It now allows businesses to buy keywords, and corporate tweets will appear when the keyword is searched for.

Currently, these ads do not appear on regular streaming. Ads will stay on the system for as long as a user clicks on it and passes it around. The principle is that relevance will rise to the top.

How do companies establish the profitability of using social media?

There may be formulations where you can establish the revenue to you from every click-in that leads to a sale. In a blog on Small Business Trends http://smallbiztrends.com/2010/05/the-social-media-money-formula.html, web marketing consultant Tyler Garns came up with a formula to figure out the profitability of social media.

It goes as such: **(R-CG)* (F*CR*OR*PR)-H*T = Profit**
Where **R** = Revenue per sale
Cg = Cost of goods
F = Number of followers/friends

Cr = Click rate (what % of followers click on your social media links and go to your site)
Or = Opt-in rate (what % of the people that clicked opted into receive info from you via email)
Pr = Purchase rate (what % of the people that opted in actually bought from you)
h = Hourly rate for your social media efforts
T = Amount of time you spend on social media

As he pointed out, this formula focuses more on the process of converting social media followers to email marketing opt-in and then seeing what percentage eventually ends up buying.

This maybe a little easier to measure for online businesses, but what about the dry cleaning chain that decides to leverage social media to get more clients?

How do you put a dollar amount on engaging your customer?

The key to social media is adding value. Ask yourself where can you add value to your customer? If you are running a dry cleaning chain, how about taking a leaf from the bargain savvy Japanese housewives, and tweeting your discounts for the day?

Don't think that social media is the panacea for all ills. There is no substitute for good old-fashioned customer service, follow-up emails, phone-calls and the thank you note or discounts on customer appreciation day.

Nonetheless, social media is a very good way to shine the spotlight on your company and your products, and a good way to generate opt-in leads. Just remember that it's a very dynamic process, and just as Facebook is constantly refining its apps, so must you when you employ social media.

The Next Chapter in Social Media?

Social media is a brutally competitive world. Now, throw into the mix location-tagging social media in the form of Foursquare, recently described as the Next Big Thing.

Is Foursquare going to revolutionize marketing and create a sub genre of proximity marketing?

As a frequent traveler, there is something to be said about checking in to a hotel, and then finding out that the pharmacy you are looking for is only just on the next street. Definitely a big time-saver from gesturing and finger pointing when attempting to communicate in a foreign language.

However, once the addictive play element has run its course, will Foursquare maintain its fans?

There are some dissenters who, after their manic check-in phase are suffering from check-in fatigue and feel that there is little else to be gained from Foursquare. In fact, these participants are starting to grouse that Foursquare ends up gaining sellable data, the merchant free advertising, but the users very little other than the digital title of mayor.

Silicon Valley heavyweight VC firm Andreessen Horowitz thinks differently. It has reversed its initial refusal to invest in Foursquare by participating in its most recent round of funding, which values it at US$95m. Pointing to a high retention rate, an increasing rate of daily check-ins and a vast market of billions of mobile phone users plus serious killer apps in the works, it feels that only good things remain in store for Foursquare.

The jury is still out on Foursquare.

What's ahead?

Social media is like web usage. Once you are engaged in it, there is no turning back. What we are seeing is really only the tip of the proverbial iceberg as so much of the world is yet to be fully wired.

India, a country of 1.2bn, has recently announced a big plan to provide broadband access to all of its 630,000 villages, no matter how far flung or remote they are.

It seeks to use the web to bridge a vast economic cultural chasm that separates the cities from the poor hamlets, and a deep caste and religion divide that festers insurgency and separatist militancy.

It has given itself till May 2012 to get every village with more than 300 residents broadband access, starting with the troubled northeast which has seen a decade of sectarian violence. As a measure of the scale of the task ahead, there are currently only 8.8 million broadband customers in India.

The potential gains – the sound of 1 billion voices newly engaged in conversation. Perhaps therein lies the secret to the success of microblogging – it's a firestarter, and conversations that may have remained unheard get a chance to be aired.

Chapter Four

Location-Based Social Media

Location-based social networking draws upon the power of GPS to enable users to share their location through their portable devices. Typically, communications stem from a mobile email or text message. Quite frequently, people use these tools to enhance their social lives, as they can not only read about new places to go, but also track where their friends are at any given time. In fact, many people use the functionality of location based social media to spontaneously get together with friends and business colleagues.

The fast growth of web phones users has expedited the growth of location based social media. People who have purchased these gadgets want to take full advantage mobile phone apps that will assist them with their day-to-day life. People with web phones, of course, want information when they are in an unfamiliar location. Whether they seek the find the nearest coffee shop to a given location, or reviews of a restaurant, details "on the go" are always quite valuable. There is a clear power and allure to relevant, real-time information.

Another reason people have gravitated to these location-based social media tools is that they enable them to combine the real and virtual worlds. For example, Foursquare enables people to compete in a competition to win "badges" at a favorite club or restaurant. When you check into a location multiple times you can earn a badge or other recognition. Certain users can also earn the title of mayor. Many have gravitated to this network because they enjoy the added benefit of playing this game that is unique to Foursquare. Instead of posting something about what they did last night, they now have the opportunity to post about what they are doing right now – and see what others are doing in the same location.

Foursquare also allows users to add "tips" to various locations including recommendations or even random thoughts. When you are near a Foursquare location, you can read other people's tips. This advice allows people to find new establishments that match their interests. Of the current, different location based social media tools; Foursquare is among the most popular. In fact, according to Inc. magazine article published July 8, 2010, Foursquare is adding 15,000 new users every day.

However, Foursquare is not without its competition, take Whrrl, for example. Whrrl is similar to Foursquare in that it offers reviews of various businesses including restaurants, stores, coffee shops etc. Whrrl users can check out these reviews via their web phones. This content is very similar to what is typically seen on Yelp, except all of the relevant details are displayed on Google maps for easy navigation. Thus, Whrrl allows users to get details about different businesses simply by clicking on them.

Whrrl differentiates itself from Foursquare, however, by allowing users to add photos as well as text with notes. This functionality gives the user the ability to tell stories. Whrrl also offers users degree of control over their privacy, as Whrrl lets users differentiate between friends and "trusted" friends. Another interesting aspect about Whrrl is that you earn points and rewards when other people save and complete your recommendations.

Loopt is another application, which actually turns your mobile device into a compass. You can see the locations where your friends have visited, along with their comments and suggestions. Loopt also can be set to alert you when your friends are near your location. Loopt is a bit different from the other tools in that it offers live tracking, so users don't have to constantly check in and announce their location. Users also have a close degree of control over how much information they want to make public.

Not surprisingly, businesses have found that they can learn a great deal about customers and their buying habits from location based social media. As a result, experts believe that these location tools will perhaps be even more valuable to businesses than regular social networking. Additionally, when people share where they are, they are publicly divulging details about products and services that they use. This gives businesses a potentially massive amount of viral exposure.

Many of these location-based social media networks are offering special programs to businesses. For example, businesses can arrange a formal partnership to attract new customers. Once you have determined who is frequenting your establishment regularly, you can use these tools to offer rewards and discounts as a further incentive to good customers.

Inc Magazine recently addressed the issue of how businesses can get involved with these social media tools in an article entitled "How to Use Location-Based Social Networks for Your Business." First of all, they suggest that companies should follow the lead of big brands that are spending money researching what will be hot. For example, Starbucks was an early adopter of Foursquare. If your company notices big businesses following a certain trend when it comes to location based social media, you should stand up and pay attention.

The Inc Magazine article also points out how business owners can directly get involved in their marketing via location based social media. Author Lou Dubois writes, "Start using the tools as an individual, monitor what customers and users are saying about your business. Then, and only then, should you start using the services for your business, as you'll have a much clearer understanding of what you need."

When business owners read comments and tips about their establishments, it can give them unique insights into how to provide more of what customers want. Further, they can respond to questions or complaints on the network, and customers will likely appreciate the interaction. Foursquare actually goes so far as to offer a special analytics service that allows companies to see the demographics of whom is checking in to their establishments. Obviously, this is a level of personal detail about customers that is highly sought after by businesses.

According to Rob Reed, an industry blogger and founder of MomentFeed.com, a company that helps companies use location-based services for marketing, is quoted as stating, "Location is growing so much faster than social media ever did. One year from now, we'll see location jump the equivalent of three years social media time." In short, the growth for location based social media is simply dramatic. Clearly, this is just the beginning for location based social media, and odds are this growth is only likely to continue.

On June 29, 2010, the New York Times published an article called "Foursquare Raises $20 Million in Venture Capital." The article explains exactly how fast Foursquare has been expanding its outreach to businesses, which now include Starbucks, Zagats, and The New York Times including over 10,000 others. The article goes on to explain, "Hyper-local is where the next big wave of mobile advertising opportunity is, because it ties into that belief that location is going to be a big enabler for marketers to more deeply engage with their customers." The idea behind hyper-local is that people will become more and more involved in reporting their ideas by writing tips and content and, in the process, they will reveal a well of detail regarding their buying habits and buying patterns.

Clearly, the tremendous investments that are currently being made as well as the huge amount of interest in location based social media means that these applications are here to stay. As more and more users adapt web phones, use of these tools will only continue to grow. With this popularity curve, there also is a unique opportunity for companies to promote their businesses and also learn valuable information about their clientele. Be sure to read the more detailed profile of Foursquare and location-based marketing in Section Three.

Chapter Five

Illustrations

Location-based marketing is changing Social Media

(Images from Foursquare)

Coupons help track your Social Media results

Skyline Comedy Cafe (Appleton, WI)
First drink is free (value up to $5) at any
show for the mayor! Print this page or
show the mobile screen version to Skyline
staff at the show to redeem your free
drink!

19th Bar (Washington, DC)
19% off your total tab/order on every third
visit!

Hey @Foursquare Mayors of Starbucks!
Show the barista you're the store mayor
& get $1 off a @Frappuccino. More info:
http://cot.ag/c7OhQZ

Starbucks
Starbucks Coffee

Consumer Starred Reviews on Yelp (by %)
(Chart courtesy of Yelp)

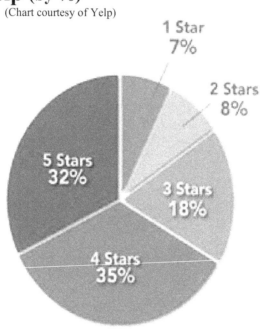

Create a Business Page on Facebook

Create a Page

Official Page

Communicate with your customers and fans by creating and maintaining an official Facebook Page.

Create a Page for a:

- ◉ **Local business:**
  - Local Business ▾
- ○ Brand, product, or organization
- ○ Artist, band, or public figure

Page name: The Star Cafe

(examples: Summer Sky Cafe, Springfield Jazz Trio)

☑ I'm the official representative of this person, business, band or product and have permission to create this Page.
Review the Facebook Terms

Create Official Page

YouTube allows you to demonstrate your expertise

Section Two

Chapter Six

Different Ways to Look at Social Media

Simple, complex, and always changing, Social Media defies easy categorization, perhaps that's why there are so many different ways to consider it.

1. Social media is a tool; it's not a plan or a strategy. A hammer cannot build a house; it doesn't know what you want to do; it is dumb, you are the smart one. Social media cannot develop a marketing campaign for you, and it is definitely not a marketing initiative all by itself.

2. Social media is not communication, it is simply another communications channel like print advertising or customer word of mouth; it is not a message in itself. As an example, commercial radio has been around for almost 100 years, but it has never sold a single product; not one. However, effective radio *copy* has sold billions of products.

3. Social media is never free, it comes with a price tag; there is a cost in terms of time and resources. You will need to plan messages, develop target key words, locate your audience, and continuously learn from your mistakes – Social Media gobbles up time if you don't have a plan.

4. There is a short list of top Social Media sites; that list is always evolving. Don't think that Social Media is all about Facebook, or you won't see the oncoming Foursquare train, notice the new MySpace redesign, or ignore the growing Tumblr.

5. Much of Social Media is for today, not next week. It has an ephemeral nature. A "tweet" is like direct response advertising, if you haven't heard from the customer within three days of your tweet, it is unlikely you ever will. Social media constantly requires new, interesting content – out of sight, out of mind. To be successful in Social Media, you must begin to think of yourself as a publisher as well as a marketer or business owner. At the same time, however, you must always remember than anything you post online never disappears and can develop a life of its own and live forever.

6. Social media is different from traditional advertising and promotion, but it is not better. It's not worse, either. The two media choices provide different benefits. It is a tool, remember? Hammer or saw? But still,

always remember that sometimes the best Social Media is a billboard.

7. Social Media can help focus your communication or send you in the wrong direction. You want to talk directly to your customers and prospects, but all too soon you justify spending time and resources communicating to people who will never be your customers. You begin to count followers rather than financial results. It is so easy to allow the power of these new media tools to overwhelm our business judgment. Your mantra should always be – stick to the plan. Focus on customers and new business; track results, not activity.

There are two sides to every story

The ancient Greeks believed that the opposite of every great idea was equally true, so it is with Social Media - the great, new idea.

8. On one hand, it gives businesses new ways to succeed in the marketplace. On the other, it also provides new ways to trip and fall flat on your face. Your mistakes can now go "viral".

9. Social media lets you gather your customers together and engage them in conversation; it also provides that same opportunity to your competitors who can become anonymous followers and join your nice, friendly conversation with your best customers. Additionally, your best customers now have a

55

method, thanks to you and social media, to talk to each other, to praise or complain about your work, or suggest alternatives to your business, in a very public forum - your social media forum.

10. No single social media tool is the right solution for all business, not even Facebook. For example, according to several research studies, Twitter is more effective than Facebook at driving foot traffic to a physical location in the real world. But Facebook has more success driving online traffic to a virtual location such as a Website. MySpace may be losing its battle with Facebook, but it might offer your business a better opportunity to be seen by the millions of users who still call My Space home. After all, Red Box is making a fortune renting DVDs – a supposedly dying market. It can all be confusing, but once you simply focus on what your customers and prospects are doing online, you know where *you* should be.

11. Social media is ironic. Most businesses get involved with social media in order to "receive" - to increase their sales -but soon realize that to be effective and gain followers or fans, they must find new ways to "give" something of value. Most often this value is provided as content – information - but sometimes value comes in another digital form, such as an app. What can you provide that has value to your target customer?

12. Ask yourself this important question, what extra bonus do my customers get when they purchase a product or service from *me*? How can you support your existing value proposition through social media?

13. There is a reason for the word "social". If you don't like social media and feel some affinity for it; it probably won't like you either. In fact, building relationships online is much more difficult than in person. If you don't want to be at the Social Media party, it will be apparent to your customers and Social Media will be just another chore that provides little in results.

Social media is only a promotional tool

14. Social media doesn't replace traditional marketing activities, it supports it. The real world still builds stronger relationships than the virtual world. You should find ways to meet your customers and prospects at "Tweet Ups" or other activities. Customers won't feel they know your company unless they know you.

The multiple facets of social media may make it seem complex. However, it gets much easier when you build a customized plan for social media marketing that is built around you, your customers, and your business. The good news is that in the final analysis, social media just requires basic marketing skills.

Chapter Seven

You, Your Business and Your Customers

Depending on your previous experience with Social Media and all of its forms, everything in this promotional channel could be new to you. If this is true for you, there might seem to be a bewildering number of Sites and applications online. In this book, we focus on the main Web tools, but there are many more. For example, Foursquare tends to dominate the discussion of location-based media, but there are nine additional companies seeking to capture this growing market. For micro-blogs, there are many more options than the ubiquitous Facebook, My Space and Twitter - although they are much smaller in comparison. But the application is not the starting point when developing a marketing plan for Social Media.

Begin with You

If you have no prior history with popular Social Media applications such as Facebook or Twitter, now is the time to begin to gain experience with these tools. To begin, you will not set up an account for your business, but instead set up a personal account (if you don't already have one) on various

Sites to begin to learn the ropes. It's okay to use a pseudonym if that makes things easier for you. You're not trying to gain followers at this point, you just want to create some "tweets", post on a Facebook wall, try to become "mayor" of a favorite business on Foursquare or put up a video on YouTube. Your choices are numerous. During this time, you're not trying to discover old friends online, but following local and national businesses to learn Social Media from a customer's perspective. The focus of this learning period is to understand fully what your customers will be doing when they interact with your business. The only way to achieve this understanding is by becoming a follower yourself. You will not only gain an understanding of how each Social Media variation that you are considering works, but you'll also get a feel for how it influences your own perceptions of other businesses that you interact with. What are they doing right? What are they doing wrong?

Unlike other types of promotions, you won't have an advertising agency or media buyer to lean on, so before you build an online presence for your business, you better understand what you are doing. How long does this learning process take? The short answer is as long as you need. It could be one month or six months (especially if you are trying divergent Medias such as starting a micro-blog or getting familiar with Foursquare).

Another aspect of this test drive is to discover the applications that seem to resonate with you. If you are confused and baffled by the "badges" on Foursquare when you are the customer, then you will probably have difficulty managing a marketing campaign that relies on building excitement around these "honors". This does not mean that you can't do anything with Foursquare, but it does indicate that you may need to find someone to handle this chore within your company. This is similar to a blogger who hates to write, but finds a ghostwriter to make posts to his blog. This may sound unwieldy, but it happens many times with consultants who have their own business blogs. They prefer to spend their time consulting and provide an outline of a blog post to a professional writer.

In the final analysis, you will probably have more success with the applications that you are comfortable with. This is not the deciding factor, of course, but it should be an important part of your planning. Very few of us do well in areas that are not in-sync with our skills or interests.

Your Business

As you begin to become comfortable with Social Media and its varied outlets, you can begin to see which applications are best-suited to your brand. If you are like most business owners that I work with, you might automatically think that you need a business page on Facebook since it is the dominant Social Media application of today. It is still too early in your learning curve, however, to make that call.

Let's create an example to illustrate that point. If you have an outdoor supply store, it is likely that you are selling your knowledge of recreational sports and your local wilderness area, as being equally valuable as the equipment such as fishing rods and camping gear that line your store shelves. If so, how will Facebook support that value proposition? Do you understand how you will create messages on a micro-blog that accomplish this?

In contrast, a business channel on YouTube *may* give you a chance to create instructional videos that showcase both your equipment and knowledge. If you tie these videos to appropriate local tags and keywords, then you'll be frequently discovered in online searches conducted by prospects in your area. Of course, you can use Facebook to drive customers and prospects to your new YouTube videos, but now your work is split between two online Medias. There is nothing wrong with using multiple channels, but you should anticipate the work involved with multiple sites.

In another section of this book, I outline the many contradictions inherent in Social Media. You may enter this channel seeking to increase business, but to succeed you will need to deliver some type of online "value" to your followers. Your media application choice should be heavily influenced by how clearly it can illustrate your value proposition to your customers and p To simplify your search, you may want to talk to a few of your best customers and ask them about their use of Social Media. Why do they use it? What applications do they use? Do they become "fans" of businesses? What are some of their favorites? Since these are your best customers, you probably have a high level of existing trust with them. Of course, be upfront in your intentions.

You should tell any customer you interview that you are researching Social Media as a potential promotional channel. If they are heavily involved with Social Media, ask them for their ideas. After all, if they know both you and Social Media, they should be a good source of information.

Finally, spend some time thinking about your customers and your value proposition. If most of your work is in the business-to-business market-place, you might want to demonstrate your added value through a traditional blog rather than a micro-blog. Once again, it doesn't necessarily mean that you won't be on Facebook, but you will be using Facebook or Twitter to alert your customers to a new blog post on your Website.

Understanding your customers is especially important when considering location based Social Media. I recently received an e-mail on my Website from a home inspector who was using Foursquare without much success. He asked for help in finding ways that he could make his Foursquare promotions relevant to his customers and prospects – not an easy task. Although you may be attracted to an application for a variety of reasons, if you cannot find a way to deliver your value message though that channel – in a manner that resonates with your customers – it is useless as a marketing tactic.

Use LinkedIn for research

I recommended that my home-inspecting reader use LinkedIn and its "Questions" feature to ask other professionals for their input. Although they might not know of a success story that directly involved home inspectors, they might know of related examples that could be "tweaked" for this reader. Right now, while Social Media is a hot topic is a great time to post questions on LinkedIn. There are literally hundreds of consultants, large and small, jockeying to become an authority in this area. One of the key ways that many experts demonstrate their expertise is through answering the questions on LinkedIn. It's a great resource to find Social Media marketing strategies that have proven to be successful in your business category – and its free to use.

Using Your Industry Contacts

As a small business, you probably know similar small business owners in non-competing markets. A few calls will typically result in finding someone, who knows someone who has mounted a successful Social Media campaign. These resources are tremendously helpful and you will benefit time and again by sharing results with non-competitors serving a similar customer base.

Weigh and Decide

With all of these inputs to your thinking, you can begin to add a certain amount of "weight" to your findings. What types of Social Media appeal to you? How much time do you have to devote to these promotions? What types of Social Media are your customers involved with now, and what are their expectations for a business using Social Media? What success stories have you uncovered from businesses in your industry? Making your final decisions on an implementation strategy is a blend of art and science, but at the end of this process you should have enough knowledge and relevant information to make an informed decision that will work for your business.

Of course, you may discover that your customers do not use Social Media. You may also realize that nothing in this digital world resonates with you. Even when you find successful examples from within your industry, you are still unmoved. In this case, there is nothing wrong with avoiding a mistake. However, if you develop a promotional strategy with potential, and that seems natural for you, your business, and your customers, you will want to calculate the potential value of your efforts and that's the subject of the next chapter.

Chapter Seven

Determining Profit with Social Media Marketing

A constant refrain in Social Media marketing is the problem in determining the return on investment for a campaign. Some of the calculations presented by various factions can be very fuzzy and differ from source to source. For example, in June of 2010, Advertising Age reported that two separate companies, Syncapse and Vitrue, had taken on the challenge of determining the value of a Facebook fan to a business page on that site. Syncapse arrived at a value of $138.38 and Vitrue claimed a far-lesser number, $3.60.

How could they both come up with such different results? The easy answer is that they are trying to measure variables that have always been difficult to define; brand loyalty, propensity to recommend, and future spending rate. But even within a mass advertising framework, these metrics have always had a certain amount of "flex". Let's take one of the measures from the report, brand affinity. A "fan" or a "like" on Facebook, according to one report, indicates greater brand affinity – but don't most fan *prospects* become actual *fans* because they already had a higher degree of brand affinity? Did Facebook create the greater brand affinity or simply help to identify and group people who processed that trait online?

The Value of "fans" and followers

The Advertising Age article also described Vitrue's process of determining the value of gathering hundreds of "likes" for a business. Vitrue used Facebook's advertising rates to develop a formula to calculate the value of an "impression" of a company's name with each member of the business's followers using a $5 CPM formula or cost per thousand impressions. The more times you post during a day and year, the greater the total value you receive. The problem with this formula is that theoretically you can receive thousands of dollars of "value" but receive nothing in terms of sales or business growth. This type of calculation is not new. It is the same rationale that NASCAR sales people use when they plaster logos on cars, uniforms, and racetrack walls to create hundreds of corporate "impressions" in a typical race. Obviously, many large corporations buy into this logic.

Advertising Age concluded its article by asking for a coordinated industry approach to determining the metrics best suited for Social Media. Ironically, this was Advertising Age which covers an industry that is still grappling with this issue after almost a century of effort. There is an old quote from a mythical ad man that is frequently quoted in advertising groups, "I know I'm wasting half of the money that I'm spending on advertising. I just don't know which half."

Measurement in advertising is really not as bad as the quote suggests, but results reporting can always become a bit unstable with any advertising executive documents results in terms of brand loyalty. As an example, Apple has legendary brand loyalty but only a small fraction of the market. Microsoft is the industry whipping boy, but still dominates due to other factors. As a further note, Apple brand loyalty is driven by product specifications, product design, and a "cool" factor that exist somewhere to the side of their advertising budget. In short, brand loyalty is not driven by advertising or Social Media marketing, but a more complex group of factors.

The best lessons on determining value come from direct marketing: this mail campaign cost $X and returned $Y in sales. Both input and output are measureable. Additionally, over time, these numbers become more precise as marketers learn how external factors such as the time of year, the economy, and creative design affect results.

Taking a lesson from direct marketing, Social Media marketing is best served simply by focusing on activities that result in measureable results. If we can accept that a business page gathers fans with greater affinity to the brand, maybe we can also accept that we won't be able to measure the effects of that brand loyalty it in a way that is particularly satisfying. It is far more productive to think of Social Media as a direct marketing channel, and create campaigns and track results in a manner that is similar to direct marketing – "I spent $X in time or resources and received $Y as a result.

Knowing Your Customers

At the beginning of this book, I wrote that a small business has an advantage compared to larger corporations in terms of Social Media. Very simply, that advantage is your customer knowledge. You already know the names and professions of your best customers – they determine a large part of your business' profitability. You take their checks, know the spouse's name, and talk to them about their interests. Depending on the type of business you run, you may know their financial situation and other confidential personal details. These people will form your core list of targeted followers for your Social Media campaign. From this base, you will target other prospective followers to add to your "A" list. Of course, others will add themselves to your list of fans, just like some customers just walk through the door without any effort on your part. However, for the best ROI, follow the established principles of direct marketing and target the mirror images of your best customers to gather new, "best" customers. It's not difficult, even without the Social Media tools listed in the resources section of part three of this book; it is easy to find anyone in a local market that is utilizing Social Media.

Targeting High Value Customers the Direct Marketing Way

All customers are not created equal. Some customers fall into what marketers refer to as a "heavy user" category. These customers purchase products or services with the highest profit margin or simply frequent your business more often than average. This important group is your most valuable asset and you probably wish you had more like them. Let's call this Group "A".

You may have also identified several other tiers within your own customer list that are responsible for lesser, but still significant, percentages of your company's profits. Although every customer is important, the customer segments making the greatest contributions to your profitability are what keep you in business. This will be Group "B" and "C". You can create, of course, as many sub-groups as seems practical.

As a rule, any well-crafted advertising message targets the most profitable customer segments – "A" by itself, or potentially "A" and "B" and "C". How many sub-segments of groups targeted depends on their profitability. Please remember this, just because you are targeting one group doesn't mean you won't see results from all three or more. To stay within our direct marketing framework, this potential result is different from direct mail, but similar to a broadcast infomercial in which someone from a totally unexpected demographic group responds to a TV advertisement. Our marketing efforts, however, focus on profitable customers. After all, what is the point of attracting unprofitable customers?

The Customer Profile

What do profitable customers look like when they are not at your business? Commonly, profitable customers are affluent, but it's not always that simple. For example, for fast-food giant, McDonald's, lower-income households may purchase at least one meal, each day of the week, at one of their restaurants. That's a lot of Big Macs!

Sometimes the profitable customer profile is very precise, not dictated by income, but by other factors. For a dry cleaner, the profile of the most profitable customers might fit a professional profile – attorneys for example. Attorneys work in one of the few professions in which suits and starched shirts are still standard-issue uniform. Also, since attorneys are often affluent, they will have spouses and families that utilize cleaning services for their own upscale clothing. In contrast, doctors may be equally, or more affluent, but spend the day in scrubs, avoiding formal clothes on the job.

These are hypothetical examples, but the more real and detailed your profile of your profitable customer segments, the more likely your targeted Social Media campaign will deliver the results you expect.

Social Media – Friends Flock Together

In direct marketing, we know that people tend to associate with others who are similar to themselves. They live in the same neighborhoods, engage in similar activities, and so on. In other words, lawyers form friendships with other lawyers, to extend our previous example. This tendency makes targeting profitable customers much easier. Your most profitable customers have already linked to their friends via Facebook or other Social Media application. As you locate and begin to "befriend" your customers, you will appear on their Facebook wall or are re-tweeted; you will be seen by prospects that are similar to your current heavy users in terms of customer profile, demographics and income. Even better, since you are targeting similar prospects, messages that are created for existing customers should work equally well for prospects fitting that profile.

Your Value Message

In the previous section, we discussed the various choices such as blogs, micro-blogs, videos and other channels that are available to you a Social Media channel, some media, such as blogs require more lengthy and detailed text narratives. Other choices, such as videos are quite different. It is very easy to become distracted by the format and forget the importance of your message and your audience. Always keep your most profitable customer segments in mind – that's your audience. You are speaking to them and their friends that mirror them in terms of demographics.

I've worked in advertising for many years and I know that business owners struggle with this. "Everyone could benefit from my product, I don't want to leave anyone out," they often say. My reply is this: I know you don't want to leave anyone out, but crafting a message that applies to everyone in every situation usually results in a message that says nothing of value or relevance to anyone. Let's look at two potential messages for a car dealership:

1. Come on down! We have new cars and used cars with easy credit and financing. Talk to us, we'll find what you're looking for.
2. We have 12 new Ford Fusion has arrived and we have zero percent financing available until the end of the month. It's Consumer Reports' Car of the Year!

I realize that these are very truncated messages, but they illustrate a point. Message #1 can apply to everyone, but is very weak in terms of targeting or creating consumer action. Message #2 is more likely to bring in people interested in a new Ford Fusion. But don't fret; the ad will also bring in folks who will end up buying a used car. It's not excluding them at all. Creating messages that bring in your most profitable customers and prospects makes the most business sense. With additional resources, you can expand your messages to other less-profitable groups.

Alternatively, If your follower base expands to include customers from several groups, you can vary your message develop to include targeted messages for those groups as well. You may want to develop some formula such as 40 percent of messages are directed to Group "A", 10 percent to Group "B" and so on.

Tracking Customers

Most customer databases are transactional in nature. They capture sales, product numbers, and customer names, etc. They do not, however, help to create messages or track results. To make results tracking efficient, you will need to attach a notational field to your customer records which makes note of their Social Media affiliation. As new customers are acquired, it is helpful if coupons or specials that the new customer might use are tracked back to a Social Media outlet, allowing you to see results over time. Also, you may be able to track results that provide some substance to the real contribution that "greater brand loyalty" of Social Media followers provide to your business.

Using the Present Value Formula

All of us in business know that there are high costs involved in acquiring a customer. But once the customer is through the door, the costs involved in maintaining a client are far lower.

Depending on your business classification, attracting new customers that match your heavy-user profile can have significant impact. Many businesses have an inherent "stickiness" to them. Once a tax accountant acquires a customer, the customer tends to remain a client for a long time due to the perceived high cost of finding a new accountant. The client believes there is value in the shared history and knowledge of his or her personal situation that cannot be easily duplicated.

Other businesses may experience more frequent customer turnover. Returning to the dry cleaners example, it is rare to find a customer who "sticks" with the same shop for a decade or more.

We use a dry cleaning business as an example here; but the concepts are universal and can apply to any business, whether you own an outdoor camping store, a pool cleaning service or a lawn mowing business. To make these examples useful, please adapt these figures to your own circumstances.

To determine the future stream of earnings (be it 1,5, or 10 years), we will use the Present Value formula which is used by value investors to calculate what a stock is worth today, and by bondholders to determine if a bond or treasury bill is worth investing in.

You should also note that "Profit" is separate from Gross Revenue. Profit is what remains after the incremental cost of operations is subtracted from revenue. In the dry cleaners example, it would be the cost of chemicals and other resources that are needed to fulfill the order for that customer. These calculations assume that expense is taken into account. Using these calculations help to determine your profit potential for a customer. Since there might not be a real dollar cost to some types of Social Media marketing, there is always a time cost. The difference between your cost in time and the profit of each new customer reveals the actual results of your marketing campaign.

If you cut away the language and specific industry references, we are all after the same thing – how much should we invest in something today to earn so much in the future?

Please note, I am assuming a longer than average retention period for a typical dry cleaning customer for illustration purposes. You should use the average customer retention period that is normal for your business. Whenever possible, always make conservative estimates to help ensure you don't spend more on each customer than they are worth to you.

What Numbers Do You Plug In?

Where your work as a business owner is concerned, you need to determine…

P – which is the profit from the customer per period. The period can be per month or per year. For simplicity, we'll use a year

N – how many years of expected earnings will you get from a committed and loyal customer? This varies, as we discussed.

i– the discount rate. In finance, it's what they call the risk-free rate or the T-bill rate.

For businesses, one of the best rates to use is your cost of capital. What are you paying the bank for a working capital loan? That's the rate to use. (Bear in mind the higher the rate, the safer and less risky are your assumptions, but the lower the Present Value.

As a formula, it might read:

$$PV= \frac{P^1}{(1+i)} + \frac{P^2}{(1+i)^2} + \frac{P^N}{(1+i)^n}$$

Case Example: A Dry Cleaning Business

Peter, your top customer is a 30 year old lawyer, and spends an average of $100 a week in having his shirts and suits dry-cleaned.

Therefore, in a 50-week year, (excluding holidays), Peter will spend $5000.

Let us assume that Peter will live close by to you for the next five years (it can be 10 or whatever number you think is realistic. If he's unmarried, the likelihood is that Peter will marry and move to the suburbs in 5 years, so let's stick with 5 for now.

On the other hand if you know that Peter is married, has bought a home, is a partner in the firm and is set to live out for the rest of his live where he is, you can work out the Present Value of his earnings for 15-20 years. The choice is yours.

But for now, we'll use 5 years and a 6% interest rate on your bank loan. On a spreadsheet, it might look like this:

Excel PV Calculation

	$	
P= Profit per year	3,000.00	Profit
N=Number of years	5	Years
i=Cost of Capital	6%	use as Discount Rate
PV	$12,637.	

Therefore, slotting the numbers into the Present Value formula, this is what it looks like:

$$PV = \frac{3000}{(1.06)} + \frac{3000}{(1.06)^2} + \frac{3000}{(1.06)^3} + \frac{3000}{(1.06)^4} + \frac{3000}{(1.06)^5}$$

And the answer is: $12,637.

If you projected this 10 years out, the number is $22,080.

You're probably wondering why it's that you get $12,637 after 5 years, and only $22,080 after 10 years.

The principle in Present Value is that there is a time decay, and money today (or as close to today) is "worth" more than money far in the future. If you have 5 premium customers like Peter, their worth to you is $12,637 X 5 = $63,185.

With time, you will have an idea of the hours that you are devoting to Social Media marketing for each new client which give you an accurate idea of your costs versus profits.

Use the Present Value Formula to Rank Clients

Let's assume the dry cleaner has 5 clients. The premium clients are Peter and his twin brother, Paul, and they have identical spending habits. Therefore, you know that 5 years' business from Peter and Paul will earn you

$12,637 X 2 = $25,274 in today's dollars.

There are 3 more clients, who started out as walk-in customers. They don't have a whole lot of dry cleaning, and you have a vague idea of the amount of business they bring. The question becomes: Is it better to spend more money to attract more premium clients like Peter and Paul, or is it better to cut costs and hope for regular walk-in clients? By knowing what you can potentially earn from them, you get a grasp of how much you'll be willing to spend.

By working out the Present Value, you can rank client segments

You notice from past behavior that one third of the walk in clients will fall away after 1 year. Therefore, you are left with 2 that may give you business for 5 years.

For client no. 1 who falls away after Year 1 and who gives you $20 of dry cleaning a month, for which $12 is profit, the Present Value formula is:

$$\underline{P}\,(1+i) = \$136.00$$

Clients 2 and 3 will give you a total of $50 a month in dry cleaning, but you can expect their business for 5 years.

The PV of their business is:

$$PV = \frac{360}{(1.06)} + \frac{360}{(1.06)^2} + \frac{360}{(1.06)^3} + \frac{360}{(1.06)^4} + \frac{360}{(1.06)^5}$$

$$= \$1,516$$

Adding all three together, clients 1, 2 and 3 will give the dry cleaners only $1,652 in business over five years, a fraction earned from premium customers like Peter and Paul.

Using the Present Value formula allows you to strategize better by improving your grasp of the following:

1. Where to spend your Social Media resources, which type of customer do you want to attract and making a decision between a "premium" strategy or a "volume" strategy.
2. With an identifiable and measureable stream of income, you are better able to figure out how much you are willing to spend today to get this future stream of income.
3. By ranking your customers, you figure out the demographics you want to concentrate on.

Need an Easier Way to Do This?

There are many online calculators that will calculate present value that you can adapt for your purposes. Remember to subtract the cost of operations.

Calculating the Value of Increased Business

New location-based applications such as Foursquare drive increased usage from among your customer base. The premise behind location-based marketing is that the marketing directly to customers with Web-enhanced cell phones will increase the frequency of their in-store visits. But how will you calculate the value of these increased visits?

One again, it simplifies calculations to focus on your customer list, sorted by profitability. Then it becomes a simple matter of calculating how incremental improvements in store visits will affect your bottom line.

Here is how this might play out on a spreadsheet if you influenced the visits and purchases of a group of customers. In this example, the group of customers spends an average of $25 per week at your business. A location based social media strategy prompts an average increase of 20 percent in visits and purchases per customer.

	Current	Increase	Adjusted
Weekly revenue	25.00	20%	$ 30.00
Incremental profit %	60%		60%
Weekly profit	$15.00		$ 18.00
Number of weeks	50		50
P=Profit per year	$750.00		$ 900.00
Period	1	Year	1
Cost of Capital	6.0%		6.0%
PV	$707.55		

$849.06

20%   increase in PV

Forward and Backward Views

The benefit of the approach that I describe here is that it allows you to make accurate projections for future profitability. As you begin to see results, you can adjust this formula, making adjustments to your projected assumptions with real world results.

Additionally, you will want to include costs that are specific to your online promotions to this group, such as coupons, discounts or other group specific programs.

Section Three

Chapter Nine

Twitter

Twitter's micro-blogging has taken the world by storm. Not just sports stars, reporters or high tech moms, it is playing a pivotal role in political events, most recently in Bangkok's anti-government uprising and reporting on shootouts and vote buying before Philippines' May elections.

Politicians have caught onto the importance of micro-messaging in 140 characters or less. However, there can be no greater acknowledgement of Twitter's impact on social culture and history than the Library of Congress' decision in March 2010 to archive public tweets. There is an ongoing flood of 55 million tweets a day, and in the four years since Twitter was created in San Francisco on March 31, 2006, it has accumulated more than 10 billion messages.

These represent a sea of history - more observations recorded in a single medium at the same time by more people than ever in history. To put it into perspective, 10 billion looks like a large number, but in the digital domain, that many tweets will take up only 5 terabytes of information. A 2 terabyte drive costs only around $150.

Despite many junk messages, Tweets preserve extraordinary accounts, especially of what its chairman Jack Dorsey describes as "massively shared experiences" made in the moment, by people all over the planet. In the recent uprising in Bangkok, the stranded, injured and the dying inside a temple were rescued after a Canadian journalist had his followers retweet his pleas for help.

Beginnings Of Tweets

Twitter's beginnings were less glorious. It was actually a side project proposed by Jack Dorsey, to board members of a podcasting company, Odeo, which was then down in the dumps. Dorsey sketched out the idea on a legal pad.

His original inspiration? Bicycle messengers, and how it is they have to be constantly squawking about where they are at any point in time.

Jack Dorsey had first tried out the idea in 2000 but it was only when technology allowed SMS to take off that the idea was again revived.

Twitter was used firstly for internal memos and a full-scale version was launched in July 2006. By October of that year, Biz Stone, Evan Williams and Dorsey, Twitter's co-founders, moved to start a new company called Obvious, which acquired Twitter.com, among other assets from Odeo.

Evan Williams already had an internet hit to his name. He had sold Blogger, a live Web journal service, to Google, which he had worked in briefly, and before starting Odeo with Stone.

The name? It was originally "twitch" but that did not carry the right imagery. When the founders came across "twitter" in the dictionary that was defined as "a short burst of inconsequential information," and "chirps from birds", they knew they had a winner.

The Take-Off Point

At the Austin-based South by Southwest music festival, Twitter staff cleverly placed large plasma screens in hallways, streaming Twitter messages. Crowds would mill around getting updates on hot parties, popular restaurants and panels to listen to. Daily volume went from 20,000 tweets to 60,000. Barely a year after its start, Newsweek in March 2007 described Twitter's brevity as the Next Big Thing.

"In the overheated world of Web 2.0, where startups bloom and spread like triffids, Twitter has become the viral craze du jour and traffic is booming," it said.

Brevity Speaks Volumes

Tweet traffic keep increasing in quantum leaps. It reached 500,000 tweets a quarter by end 2007, By the end of 2008, the corresponding number was100 million tweets. That year, Fortune called Twitter " the hottest web startup."

The numbers have continued to rise in a vertical straight line; in the first 3 months of 2010, 4 billion tweets had been sent from 100 million users.

Approximately 300,000 users are added each day and more than 70,000 apps have been created to work with Twitter.

The New York Times in addressing the question of "How Twitter will Change your Life" eloquently pointed out that injecting Twitter into social interaction and conversation "fundamentally changed the rules of engagement."

At its start, Twitter users were answering "What are you doing?", the question that started a media revolution. However, in late 2009, reflecting a change in focus from personal updates to news and the beginning of a new advertising strategy, Twitter posed a new question, "What's happening?"

Untold Amounts of Financing

Although Twitter has cut some revenue deals, estimated at US$25m annually, with Google, Microsoft and Yahoo, to license its stream of microblogs it never really had a revenue model to capitalize on its exponential growth.

However, that strategy has changed. It is to launch Promoted Tweets, which will dish up ads in users' feeds that will match keywords that Twitterers use in their search. The third source of revenue will be the yet to be launched commercial accounts, which require business users to pay for services such as detailed analytics.

There were early signs of the winds of changing blowing through. In 2008, Dorsey stepped down as CEO and became Twitter's chairman, while co-founder Jack Stone became CEO. Never one for acquisitions previously, it bought a search engine company, Summize, in 2008 to build out its search capabilities. In 2010, it bought out Tweetie from Atebites, which makes a Twitter app for the Iphone.

As a private company, Twitter is tight-lipped about money it has raised. It had two undisclosed rounds of capital raising in 2007 and 2008 from investors such as Jeff Bezos of Amazon. In 2009, it received $35 million from a number of venture capital firms including Benchmark Capital, with the total raised to date estimated by Business Week at $150 million.

What are Tweets Worth?

There is no official valuation of Twitter, but in 2008, Facebook allegedly offered $500 million of its own stock to acquire Twitter. The offer was declined. Sharespost, which makes a secondary market in private equity shares, this year, valued Twitter at $ 1.4 billion.

Twitter's decision to accept advertising revenues is the first move to capitalize on the audience it has captured. It is as important a change as when Google started taking in ads. How much are the tweets really worth? No one knows at this point, but perhaps the IPO which is said to be "in the distant horizon" according to its COO, Dick Costolo, may answer the question sooner than expected.

Chapter Ten

Facebook

It is difficult for most people today to imagine the Internet without the all-encompassing presence of Facebook. In just a few short years, Facebook has transformed from relative obscurity to a Website that is considered one of the most popular in the world. In fact, the Internet ranking system Alexa considers Facebook to be the second most visited website. Only Google now generates more traffic than the ever-growing Facebook.

Much of the Facebook's success can be traced to the fact that it was seen as an alternative to such other social networking sites like MySpace. For those seeking an alternative, Facebook was a natural solution. There were numerous reasons that people were eager to switch over from MySpace. Facebook offered a smooth and organized interface, as opposed to MySpace, which many users found to be visually unappealing. Also Facebook tended to appeal more to adults: whereas, MySpace had the reputation of being for younger people.

Facebook was the brainchild of Mark Zuckerberg who developed the concept while at Harvard. In fact, the Facebook concept developed out of an early concept called Facemash. The Facemash idea was designed so that users could rank the attractiveness level of fellow Harvard students. However, in order to accomplish this feat, Zuckerberg illegally accessed Harvard's computer network and took the necessary images.

Facemash was an overnight success. Yet, once Harvard officials discovered the Website they immediate shut it down. Quite amazingly, all legal charges were dropped against Zuckerberg who also was given permission to remain a student at Harvard.

Zuckerberg, however, now knew that he was onto something and believed that his concept could be expanded. By early 2004, Zuckerberg was hard at work developing what would be called "thefacebook." Thefacebook.com was launched by February 2004. Thanks in part to the word of mouth, news of the new website spread quickly throughout the Harvard student body.

Soon thefacebook had expanded to other colleges and universities. In fact, it is safe to state that the speed at which Facebook's presence expanded in 2004 was quite remarkable.

Just a year later, Facebook was incorporated. Sean Parker was named as the company's president, and operations were relocated to Palo Alto, California. Originally Parker was simply an adviser for Zuckerman, but as the site progressed, he brought his expertise on full-time as the company's president. Sean Parker was a cofounder of the once highly popular music site, Napster. As a result of his time with Napster, Parker was very familiar with all things Internet and was quick to see the potential of Facebook.

Almost from the beginning, Facebook has been engulfed in lawsuits of various sorts. One high profile example comes from several Zuckerberg classmates who claimed to have had a hand in the development of the site. They claim that Zuckerberg stole their concept and violated a verbal agreement. There are reports that a settlement was reached between the parties.

Restricted access was a major part of the initial Facebook concept. While the website was still called thefacebook, as it wasn't until 2005 that the Facebook.com domain was obtained, access was restricted to a handful of Ivy League universities. Slowly, more universities were allowed into the social networking site. Eventually a few of America's largest companies such as Microsoft were included.

By May 2005, major press outlets such as the New York Times had begun to take serious notice of Facebook, running a promotional piece for the website stating, "The site is becoming ubiquitous at the 840 colleges where it is available." By the time this New York Times article was written in 2005, Facebook had already had over 2.8 million registered users located throughout over 800 college campuses.

It was not until the fall of 2006, that the average person could join Facebook. Since that time, Facebook has nearly taken over the Internet and now dominates the social networking scene. Today, Facebook dominates social networking on the web with some notable exceptions. For example, there are regional exceptions as exemplified by Orkut in Brazil and Hyves in The Netherlands, among many others. Yet, there is no denying that Facebook is the dominant player in the global social networking game.

Facebook has had very little trouble finding funding over the years. Zuckerberg's creation received its first major investor in the form of Internet giant Peter Thiel, founder of PayPal, who invested in Facebook in 2004. Since that time, Facebook has enjoyed a constant stream of investment.

The website's actual value is clearly in the billions. Facebook walked away from a $1 billion dollar deal with Yahoo! in 2006. There have been rumors of additional negotiations with other parties that may have reached far higher offering prices. In fact, Forbes Magazine pointed out in December 2009 that estimates have determined that Facebook is worth about $11 billion. This figure is based on the amount of money that people are willing to pay for shares of the company.

By June of 2009, Facebook had done what would have initially seemed to be impossible; it had bested MySpace. MySpace was once the dominant player in social networking and had the muscle of Rupert Murdoch behind it. By 2009, reports were that Facebook had passed MySpace for total users. In fact, in June 2009, The Los Angeles Times wrote an article called "Facebook Dethrones MySpace in the US" which stated, "The Palo Alto, Calif., company had 70.28 million users last month, topping MySpace's 70.26 million, ComScore said. Facebook's users almost doubled from a year earlier, while MySpace lost 5%." This trend of users leaving MySpace and switching to Facebook continues to this day.

What does the future of the site hold? Increasingly, there are concerns that Facebook may not be handling users privacy in an appropriate manner. A May 19, 2010 article in the Wall Street Journal entitled "Facebook Grapples with Privacy Issues" pointed out this growing concern. The article's writer Jessica E. Vascellaro noted that people are becoming increasingly concerned about Facebook and its perception of privacy due to "embarrassing technical glitches that exposed personal data." This article goes on to state, "The site's privacy travails have rattled Facebook employees and put pressure on Mr. Zuckerberg, who has argued for years that its users should be more open with their information."

Will these concerns over lack of privacy be the undoing of Facebook? This is impossible to say. But there is no denying this website's growing power. Currently, the site has a half a billion registered members and is still growing on a day-to-day basis.

Chapter 11

Linked In

Silicon-Valley based LinkedIn had pretty much the same iconic start that high-tech legends are made of. The only differences were that rather than being a college dropout, its major founder and current chairman, Reid Hoffman, was an Oxford-trained philosopher, and it was started in his living room, and not his garage.

Sitting in the living room in 2002 at the birth of the concept of a professional social network were Hoffman, Allen Blue, Jean-Luc Vaillannt, Eric Ly and Konstantin Guericke. Hoffman had prior to that time worked in Apple, Fujitsu, and as its executive vice-president, helped sell PayPal to ebay in 2002.

LinkedIn went live on May 5, 2003, a day cheekily renamed by its staff as Cinco de LinkedIn, with its five founders and 350 of their friends. By month end, it had 4,500 members. The momentum continued unimpeded and in less than 6 months of its start, it had secured its first external investor.

Mark Kvamme, partner of well-known Silicon Valley venture capital firm, Sequoia Capital, explained that their $4.7 million financing was motivated by the "patented and effective technology that has the power to transform hiring", in a leading edge manner reminiscent of the way PayPal re-engineered the transfer of money. By the end of

2003, LinkedIn's membership had grown to 81,000, and a staff of 14 employees.

An Era of Rapid Growth

LinkedIn achieved its first major milestone, boasting a roll call of half a million members in April 2004, just a little shy of its first birthday. Its second round of financing, of $10 million, was led by Greylock, an early-stage investor that has a reputation of leading the most number of its investments to IPO status. Other LinkedIn investors at this stage looked like a who's who of Silicon Valley including Netscape co-founder Marc Andressen and Peter Thiel, co-founder of PayPal.

From 1.6m members at the end of 2004, half of which were internationally based, LinkedIn catapulted to reach a membership count of 4 million at the end of 2005. Many firsts were launched in 2005:

- LinkedIn Jobs, its first premium service, which leverages members' networks to finding job opportunities, was introduced in March
- A paid subscription service open to recruiters, headhunters, personnel directors, sales firms and businesses to find the best talent.
-

By 2007, LinkedIn had reached the tipping point, with more than 9 million members, a presence in 120 different types of industries, huge strides that led USA Today to describe LinkedIn as "a giant" in the networking industry.

Its community included 3,200 publicly traded companies and 4,400 private businesses, testifying to the business world's recognition of how LinkedIn had revolutionized the business of hiring and recruiting.

Another milestone: LinkedIn became profitable with earnings derived from ad revenues, premium subscriptions and corporate solutions, where companies can create their own profiles.

Flip-Flop

The following year, 2008, was a year of many changes and leaps forward. It formed several strategic alliances with New York Times, CNBC and Business Week to distribute news content tailored to their members' profiles, opened its first international office in London, launched a French version, and ended the year with 33 million members.

However, it was also a year when Facebook's tremendous popularity raised questions about LinkedIn's future. Facebook was seen as the poster child of social networking, a perception accented by Microsoft's purchase of a tiny 1.6% stake for $240 million.

There was a schism in public opinion about LinkedIn's prospects which was echoed by the New York Times. Just as one of its reports in August 2008 was questioning if LinkedIn was "socially relevant", another report described it as "the ultimate rodolex" at a time when the financial and economic tsunami was leaving millions stranded and unemployed.

LinkedIn itself was not spared from the aftermath of the economic recession. In November of that year, it laid off 10% of its staff to refocus on revenue growth and to maintain positive cash flow. However, several rounds of financing totaling $75 million from investors such as Goldman Sachs and Bessemer Ventures, placed LinkedIn in a strong position which Business Week described as "Recession Ready".

Between December 2008 and July 2009, LinkedIn went through three changes of CEOs, as the company flip-flopped as to what it wanted to be – a Facebook for the working professional or a network for experts.

With a new CEO, Jeff Weiner of Yahoo, refocusing on its revenue formula, (revenues were up 50% over the previous year), LinkedIn continued to its spree of releasing new applications - for Palm, IBM Lotus, Microsoft, a global application for Blackberry. It also launched a German version, and opened an office in Amsterdam.

Importantly, it partnered with Twitter to share information across platforms. For LinkedIn, its end goal was to lasso in the professional information that was shared on Twitter to its user base, and to be seen as the hub of professional conversation. Tweets now appear next to the LinkedIn profiles, as the two collaborate to take relationship building to the next level.

Going Forward

LinkedIn is now firmly acknowledged as the go-to destination for professionals, a sentiment echoed by Fortune Magazine which, in its March 2010 cover story, featured LinkedIn as the only social site to "fire up your career."

The CEOs of the Fortune 500 companies have their profiles on LinkedIn, members now number 65 million in 170 countries and a new LinkedIn profile is created every 2 seconds.

LinkedIn remains a private company, but Sharespost, which creates a secondary market in private equity stakes, recently valued the company at approximately $1.3 billion, compared with $1.4 billion for Twitter and $11.5 billion for Facebook. Not too bad for a seven year old company conceived on "the theory of small gifts" which is a belief dear to Reid Hoffman.

In a past interview, Hoffman, who switched from academia to business to make the world "a nobler place" said, "When you're embedded in an ecosystem, it makes sense for you to think of little tiny things you can do for other people, things that can have huge value for them."

"If you can create structures where the interests of millions of align with the group's interest, then you can actually create things that generate a lot of value in the system."

Chapter 12

YouTube

Many people simply can't imagine a time without YouTube, but the fact is that this video-sharing site has only been in existence since early 2005. In just a few short years, YouTube has gone from newcomer to dominator. In the realm of video-sharing, few sites can even come close to matching YouTube. Like its parent company Google, YouTube dominates on the web.

YouTube was designed to be a place where people are free to upload content. Much of the content that is loaded onto YouTube's website is material from copyrighted television and movie programs. This aspect of the site has received a great deal of attention. However, copyrighted material is far from being the only type of content on YouTube. In fact, the scope and variety of content that is showcased on this website is nothing short of staggering. This is due, in part, to the fact that YouTube is available in fourteen different languages.

People are using YouTube for everything from promoting their own products and video blogging to showcasing their independent films and animations. YouTube is even used by major media outlets and news organizations to promote their content. By 2008, YouTube had agreements with companies such as CBS and Lions Gate Entertainment where television shows and films could legally be posted to the site. As of 2010, YouTube has formed over 10,000 content partners in total from around the world.

YouTube was developed and launched by former PayPal employees Steve Chen, Chad Hurley and Jawed Karim. Chen and Karim were both from a computer science background and developed the site in response to problems they had experienced involving sharing videos over the web. Interestingly, Steve Chen was also one of the first employees at Facebook, but left the company to pursue his YouTube plans. Chad Hurley was instrumental in the creation of the company's logo.

The real breakthrough for YouTube and its young founders came in late 2005, when they were able to secure over $11 million in funding from Sequoia Capital. Sequoia Capital is the same venture capital fund that has played a role in numerous Internet start-ups, including PayPal and LinkedIn.

After several months of work, YouTube officially launched a beta site in May of 2005. The rate of growth for the site was nothing short of phenomenal. Within just one year, YouTube was experiencing an impressive 100 million videos being viewed each day. Even while it was still a new website, the potential of YouTube was clear to many people. Mashable.com wrote an article in 2005 entitled, "YouTube-The King of Video Sharing?" Quoting Nathan Weinberg of Inside Google, Mashable stated, "YouTube has moved ahead of Google Video in terms of popularity...But its not just Google-these guys have moved ahead of everybody!" Even in 2005, industry insiders realized that Google was going to be the dominant player in video searches and video downloads.

Part of what makes the YouTube story such a fascinating one is how website grew with such unprecedented speed. By 2006, it was a dominant player in the video download game. In October 2006, Internet giant Google acquired YouTube for a whopping $1.65 billion dollars, which was paid in Google stock.

With the help of Google, YouTube has found yet more growth. By 2010, a remarkable two billion videos are served each and every day. In fact, the amount of content that YouTube has at its disposal is likely to play a significant role in the development of Google TV.

There are many video-sharing sites on the web, but YouTube quickly managed to distinguish itself. Part of what makes YouTube somewhat unique is this wide spectrum of diversity. Today, YouTube is used for just about every reason imaginable. You can quickly find videos from media giants like CBS or children's piano recitals for grandparents and relatives to watch worldwide.

YouTube also began providing a method through which users could profit from their videos. As of 2007, YouTube has allowed users to place advertisements in and around the videos they upload. The money from these ads is then split between YouTube and the user. In 2008, Brian Stelter at The New York Times wrote an article entitled, "YouTube Videos Pull in Real Money." This article explains how people are able to make a living through adding advertising to the YouTube videos they produce. Buckey writes, "One year after You-Tube, the online video powerhouse, invited members to become 'partners' and added advertising to their videos, the most successful users are earning six-figure incomes from the website."

Of course, the site has not been without its controversy. On one level, the site has been attacked for not doing enough to combat copyright infringement on the site. The issue of copyright on You-Tube, of course, reached a fevered pitch when Viacom sued YouTube. Not surprisingly, this resulted in a very messy legal battle.

Google, the parent company of YouTube, even went so far as to state that Viacom had uploaded large volumes of its own content on purpose. Wired Magazine covered this issue in a March 18th, 2010 article called "Accusations Fly in Viacom, You-Tube Copyright Flight." The article includes a quote from Google stating, "'Viacom alone has uploaded thousands of videos to YouTube to market hundreds of its programs and movies, including many that are works in suite,' Google wrote. 'Given the broad scope of marketing, YouTube could not be charged with knowledge of infringement merely because it came across a video that was clearly from a professionally produced television show or movie."

Yet this is only one aspect of the legal problems that YouTube has faced. Several countries, including China and Pakistan, have shut down the site for a variety of political reasons. However despite its problems, YouTube has grown seemingly unabated.

YouTube realized the high-definition would be an important aspect of the site, and with this fact in mind has slowly moved the site in this direction. In November 2008, 720p HD was added as an option for videos and full 1080p quality was added about one year later. By 2009, some 3D content was made available as well.

As of 2010, YouTube held an Alexa ranking of 3rd of all sites on the Internet. Part of this success stems from the sites incredible 23 page views per visitor. YouTube visitors average about twenty minutes on the site per visit. These incredible numbers are further amplified when one considers that YouTube's parent company is Google, whose Alexa ranking is number one. Thus, with the acquisition of YouTube, Google effectively gained the spot of both number one and number three of all Internet web destinations.

Few sites have ever experienced the rate of growth that YouTube has experienced and continues to experience to this day. Today, billions of videos are watched daily on the site, and there seems to be no stopping YouTube's growth. The simple fact is that YouTube has become a vital part of many people's lives. The site is truly nothing short of a global phenomenon. In recent years, YouTube has been taking serious steps towards monetizing the site, and there is little doubt that parent company Google will likely earn back far more than it initially invested.

Chapter 13

Foursquare

It's hip to be square. Foursquare that is. More than 1 million global, avid subscribers think so of the location-based mobile networking service. Just slightly more than a year old, Foursquare's worth is valued at $125 million if the rumor mills are right about the offer from Yahoo. As well, two powerful Silicon Valley venture capital firms, Andreessen Horowitz and Khosla Ventures, have lurked at the perimeters, offering sizeable deals around $100 million. New York-based Foursquare has drawn new subscribers far more rapidly than Twitter, no mean achievement, but the triple digit million dollar offers are given without the company earning a single cent of revenue. Yet because of Foursquare, terms like "Mayor" and "Swarm" have been introduced into the lexicon of pop culture.

Foursquare is a social networking application available on the iPhone, BlackBerry, Android, and webOS mobile phone operating systems. According to Dennis Crowley, the company co-founder, "Foursquare is a little bit of everything – a friend-finder, a local city guide, and an interactive mobile game." When a patron visits your brick and mortar business, the GPS capabilities of the phone allow the user to tell their friends where they are. As patrons "check-in" at your business through the application, they are awarded points and badges which are displayed on their profile, sent to all their friends, and posted on the front-page of Foursquare. But, it's more than just a GPS. It's also a competitive game, with players vying to be the most regular of your customers. For this reason, Foursquare can encourage repeat visitors. The patron who visits your store the most often in a two month period becomes "Mayor" of your business in the Foursquare universe. For some, these badges, titles, and achievements become addictive incentives to return to your venue. What is the story behind this hot technology story which MSNBC.com describes as the next big thing as it poses the question "Is Foursquare the New Facebook?"

The Beginnings

Foursquare was started in New York by Dennis Crowley and Naveen Selvadurai at Think Coffee, a fair-trade joint on Bleeker Street. Were their good fortunes foretold in the coffee dregs as they downed caffeine and sketched out the architecture of this part friend finder, part social city guide and part addictive nightlife game?

It started as a nightlife game, but its popularity has extended so far and wide that you can now earn virtual merit badges as Mayor of Detroit Airport or your dog can become head pooch of Central Park in New York City.

Crowley was the brains behind Dodgeball, a similar system which he sold to Google in 2006. Google shut down Dodgeball in 2009.

When Foursquare was introduced at the South by Southwest Interactive (SXSWi) in Austin, which is now a mecca for social networking hipsters and visionaries, it was acknowledged to be the belle of the ball. With a global rollout in cities in South America, Asia, Australia, Africa, Europe, and the Middle East, it is now seen as the Next Big Thing. Altogether, Foursquare is in more than 100 cities.

Foursquare works because GPS-enabled smartphones are much more widely used than they were during Dodgeball's time. It is available as an app on the iPhone, Blackberry, Android phones, Palm's Pre and Pixi. Now by checking in on your smart mobile, your friends can find where you, what you are doing, what you are recommending and what surprises they may be missing out on.

Foursquare devotees are dedicated, if not fanatical, to the service. Hundreds of parties were held from East to West Coast to celebrate the first Foursquare Day - 4/16, got it? -, which was not even their official first birthday. However, Foursquare was only too happy to give the stamp of approval to these parties, and hosted their own rooftop bash, where partygoers were rewarded with the virtual Foursquare badge, a sign of ultimate cool.

Before Foursquare

CEO Crowley graduated from Syracuse University in 1999 and ended up working with Jupiter Research, a tech-analysis firm. Like his colleagues, Crowley was young with plenty of disposal income, but soon realized it was hard work to have a fun social life, and there had to be a better way to find out where the next party was being held. He later joined a firm which developed a city guide app for Palm Pilot, which was eventually sold to a Japanese company.

However, 9/11 happened, Crowley was evicted from his apartment, and after finding work as a snowboarding instructor, he completed his Masters in New York University. There he met Alex Rainert, with whom he developed Dodgeball.

Foursquare co-founder Selvadurai, arrived at the same destination of desiring a geo-location app, by taking a slightly different route. He was the lead architect of a location based firm called Socialight, prior to which he had spent years in mobile programming for Sony. However, Selvadurai had also put in time travelling through Asia and contemplating geo-tagging, the benefits of which were brought home to him in Tokyo.

On a cold winter day in 2002, Selvadurai wandered around Akihabara, Tokyo's bustling electronic district, in search of a legendary videogame store called Super Potato. He spent hours looking for it and was just about to throw it in when he finally stumbled across the six-story arcade. He realized this was something he could have avoided, had it been geo-tagged.

Moving Forward with Life as A Game

It has been a whirlwind for Foursquare. When Google shut Dodgeball down in January 2009, Crowley swore to come up with a similar system, and did so two months later. His motivation behind Foursquare was "how do you find out the good things to do, who to meet up with next, how to have the best experience," he has said in press interviews.

"We make tools that make your social life more interesting and efficient," in line with his vision to have Foursquare as developing beyond a nightlife game into a "service that encourages people to do new things and get rewarded."

Exploding Valuations

Shortly after its SXSWi debut, it raised $1.35 million in funding in August by Union Square Ventures, which had previously invested in Twitter and Meetup. This funding placed a worth of $6 million on Foursquare. Other participants in this round of financing were Kevin Rose, founder of Digg, the social news site, Jack Dorsey, co-founder of Twitter; and Ron Conway, a savvy angel investor who had put money in Google and PayPal.

Valuations have exploded since. Part of that is due to the addictive and competitive game element, part due to the fact that frequent customers at businesses (who earn badges of merit) are able to tap into discounts or virtual coupons, and tell their friends about it, and part due to the growing recognition of the power of location based networking.

Geo-Based Social Networking to Burst On the Scene

Social networking linked to location through GPS coordinates is bursting on the scene, and seems to have untold potential for advertisers, especially at the level of the local community. In a recent article, New York Times wrote that local businesses need to understand the game changing environment. They now have to manage their online reputations and to promote them in social medial by engaging with with tech-savvy consumers.

If checking in becomes a mainstream activity, mobile advertising, now still a tiny percentage of overall spending on online ads, could be stratospheric levels. Proximity marketing could well be the direction of the future - after all isn't it about location, location, location? Foursquare delivers that very nicely, and advertisers are starting to hop onto to mobile social networking systems for more precision marketing.

As a location tool, Foursquare is really simple. The demographics show that users are 20 to early 30s, with increasing adoption by college students, but also include parents who use this to check in on their kids, or to put together an impromptu playground date.

Foursquare is the frontrunner in this hot race, but snapping at its heels are Gowalla, Twitter and Facebook, the latter two having announced that they are developing location-based features. However, Wired UK is acknowledging Foursquare as top gun. In its June 2010 issue, Wired had Crowley on its cover with a crown on his head, lauding him as 'The New King of Social Media."

Mayors, Businesses and Early Adopters

As a business, it hasn't done much by way of making money, but some revenue-generation strategies are being implemented. As it is, many companies have offered deals for loyal customers.

Early adopters include Starbucks, notable for being the first to have a national "mayor" special, BARTS San Francisco, the transit agency, which gives away promotional tickets for riders who check in at Bart stations, and Metro Canada, a free number one daily which delivers "location-specific editorial content" to its Foursquare service. Therefore, Foursquare subscribers will receive an alert when they are close to a store that Metro has reviewed and even link through to the full review on the Metro website.

Another key early adopter was Bravo TV whose urban fan base meshes nicely with Foursquare's users. Bravo TV launched its own page on Foursquare in January 2010 where contestants from its popular reality shows were posting tips. The History Channel has followed suit by offering historically relevant facts to users when they check into a noteworthy building.

Old line media companies such as the Wall Street Journal and New York Times are doing the same. Wall Street Journal has teamed up with Foursquare to offer banker badges to those who check in at the financial district, and a lunchbox badge for those who visit restaurants it has reviewed. Even the staid Financial Times is partnering with Foursquare to give away limited free subscriptions, in a deal to reach out to younger, more tech-savvy potential readers.

The use of Foursquare is not limited to businesses. Academic institutions as Harvard have embraced the location-based service, encouraging its students to earn a Harvard badge by sharing tips about campus venues. Harvard also delivers on and off campus info to encourage students and visitors to explore. UNC Charlotte, which was the first university to introduce on-campus location-based social networking specials, gave away free t-shirts to students who checked in at certain sports games and other University events.

A Marketing Dream

Geo-location plus gaming technology are the "it" tools now being used to connect people in the physical world. To a marketer, this is a dream come true - a real-time social networking that logs information about customer's eating, shopping habits and preferences. Through geo-based social networking, advertisers can find out exactly who their customers were, what they are doing, at any point in time.

Foursquare understands that their information is valuable. It provides a business dimension to their service, which allows business owners to track customer activity at their business, addressing the fundamental problem of calculating ROI in Social Media marketing. Owners have access to real-time venue statistics, including data about peak check in times, the gender make-up of customers, who were the most recent and most frequent customers, and which Foursquare user sent their check-in to their Twitter and Facebook accounts - basically word of mouth done digitally.

Marketing agencies make it their business to be able to track, and also manage, word of mouth. In its April 2010 issue, global consulting firm McKinsey & Company found that word-of-mouth was responsible for as such as 20-50% of all purchasing decisions. And because of the digital revolution, the old rules no longer apply.

Word of mouth no longer operates as a one-to-one communication; it's now one to many. Further, the power to sway purchasing decisions rests with a small group of elite influencers. Only 8-10% of consumers fall into this grouping, but they are four times more powerful than any other factor in influencing a buying decision.

Connecting the Dots - People to Location

Perhaps, Foursquare's appeal can be summed up by the words of Damian Bazadona, president of Situation Interactive, the digital marketing firm which has managed Twitter's campaigns. He said that in the next twelve months, "there will be a lot of movement on this notion of connecting with people based on where they are. To me, the opportunity is that moment when someone walks in or out of a venue, when they are in their high, to capture their high. Foursquare provides that opportunity."

Soon, Foursquare devotees will be able to wear their pride on their chest – in form of a Foursquare t-shirts, real pins for their baseball caps or jackets, based on the playful and colorful designs of the virtual badges. These will be sold through the Foursquare online store.

The Huffington Post, acknowledging Foursquare's spreading social and cultural influence, has written an online primer on the Foursquare virtual merit badges, which range in variety from lowly beginner to gym rat, player please to the iconic Super Mayor, and loads of titles in between.

Foursquare attracts 15,000 subscribers a week, most of whom are probably following the path of New York Times writer and user Emily Wolfe who describes it as "planned serendipity." She neither texts nor calls her friends to find out where they are, she checks into Foursquare instead.

Chapter 14

Online Resources

The Internet is flooded with online tools that let you find "followers" (prospects), measure your impact, and monitor what your customers are saying about you online (reputation management). Most of these tools are free, some offer enhanced services for an additional fee. Each are typically found in the dot.com version of their company name. Once you decide on the Social Media platform that you intend to use (YouTube, Twitter, etc.), you can visit the resources that are appropriate to your needs and goals. Some of these resources might fit into multiple categories.

Video Sites
Wetoku
Skype
yfrog
Twitvid
You Tube
Screenjelly
Jing
Flickr
Blip TV
Viddler
Kaltura
Tube Mogul

USTREAM

e Newsletters
Constant Contact
iContact
eNewslettersonline
Jango Mail

Mobile Marketing
City Search
Yelp
Yahoo
Insider Pages
Yellowbot
City Squares
Judy's Book
Mojopages
Kudzu
Userinstinct
Google Places
CityVoter
Merchant Circle
Openlist
Yellowbook
Superpages
Local
dexknows
InfoUSA
wcities
YellowUSA

MagicYellow
Zoominfo
Get Fave
hot frog
Angie's List

Social Media Sites
BeBo
Blogger
Brightkite
Delicious
Diigo
Facebook
Flickr
freado
FriendFeed
Friendster
Google Buzz
Jaiku
Koornk
LinkedIn
Multiply
My Space
myYearbook
Ning
Photobucket
Plaxo Pulse
Plurk
Posterous
Present.ly
ShoutEm

Status Net
StreetMavens
Tumblr
Twitter
TypePad
Vox
WordPress
Xanga
Yahoo Meme
Yahoo Profiles
Yammer
you are
Foursquare

Bookmarks
Digg
Delicious
StumbleUpon
Evri
Reddit
Mixx
Propeller
Diigo

Social Media Monitoring Services

Alterian
Attentio

BrandsEye
Buzz Logic
DNA 13
Radian6
Scout Labs
Spiral16
Sysomos
Google Insights
Google Trends
Bing Twitter Search
Blogpulse
Board Tracker
Copernic
Collecta
Keotag
Social Mention
Trendrr
Your Open Book
Blog Grader
Website Grader
Square Grader
Action Grader
Facebook Grader
PeopleBrowsr

Twitter Tools
Tweepsearch
Twellow
Hootsuite
SocialOomph
Tweet Deck

Twitter Grader
Flicker
Compfight
FriendorFollow
Twitter Karma
Twitter Cleaner
unTweeps

Blog Sites
Blogger
Posterous
Typepad
Wordpress

**Location Based Social Net-
works**
BrightKite
Buzzd
DeHood
Foursquare
Gowalla
Loopt
My Town
Scyngr
ShopKick
WeReward

Crowd Sourcing
Crowd Campaign
Poll Daddy

Dashboards
Twitter Dashboards
CoTweet
FriendFeed
HootSuite
NetVibes
Sentiment Metrics
SpredFast
SocialRadar
TruPulse
TweetDeck
Tweetie
Twhirl
Twitterific
ViralHeat

QA Sites
Aardvark
PeerPong
Quora
Stack Overflow

Measuring Networks
BackTweets
Klout
Twiangulate

Free Tools
BackType
BuzzGain
Cision Social Media

FiltrBox
HowSociable
Objective Marketer
Sentiment Metrics
Social Mention
Techrigy
TNS Cymfony
Trackur
Trendrr
Tweetwally
Visible Technologies
Whos Talking
Yack Track

Event Organizing
Pingg
Doodle

Retail
Foursquare
Restaurants
OpenTable

www.ingramcontent.com/pod-product-compliance
Lightning Source LLC
Chambersburg PA
CBHW021146070326
40689CB00044B/1142